THE RETURN OF JESUS CHRIST

THE
RETURN OF
JESUS CHRIST

G. T. MANLEY

INTER-VARSITY PRESS

ⓒ INTER-VARSITY PRESS

Inter-Varsity Fellowship
39 Bedford Square, London WC1B 3EY

First Edition	.	March 1960
Reprinted		September 1961
Reprinted		May 1964
Reprinted		September 1967
Reprinted		September 1969
Reprinted		April 1972

ISBN 0 85110 358 8

Printed in Great Britain by
COMPTON PRINTING LIMITED
London and Aylesbury

CONTENTS

PREFACE

THIS book has been written in response to the request for a study of the Second Advent which would be helpful to young Christians. My aim has been to confirm belief in our Lord's promise to return, to show how, in the early Church, this was a 'lively hope' which profoundly affected its life, and so to create in the Christian reader of today a love of His 'appearing'. Whilst it was in preparation a young Oxford graduate commented in a letter, ' What a cheering subject to write a book about!' Such indeed I have found it to be.

The conception of Christ's personal and visible return to earth is by no means free from difficulty. I have given space to this in chapter IV where I have tried to show that the difficulties are not insuperable, nor have they prevented great thinkers in all ages from taking the Lord's promise literally. In recent years many books have been written upon this subject of the Second Advent and what may follow. Some of these are by evangelical writers; they discuss such problems as the teaching of the Book of Revelation, the meaning of Old Testament prophecy, and the interpretation of the Millennium. Others are by liberal writers, some of whom cast doubt upon the veracity of the Bible and seek to re-interpret its message in accordance with pre-conceived ideas of the 'Church', or of the 'modern mind'. The full discussion of these differing views is aside from my purpose, but it has seemed necessary to make some reference to them, and especially to the former; for from them there is much to learn.

I am aware that on some controverted matters many of my friends would have preferred a more definite expression of opinion on my part. But it seems to me that, in treating those aspects of the subject on which equally devout Christian interpreters differ so widely, caution is necessary. I must therefore ask the reader's forbearance in this matter. Where I have ventured upon opinions, however, some readers will no doubt disagree. Let me say, therefore, that I accept sole responsibility for the views expressed and admit that I am as liable to mistake as any other. The future may reveal much which is now obscure.

In the course of my study two things have been impressed upon me. First, the Advent is everywhere regarded in the New Testament as having a present and practical bearing upon the Christian life; we must be active in the Lord's work, alert, ready and expectant. Second, it is also intensely personal. Whether the writer be Paul or Peter or John, he is looking forward with intense desire to the time when he himself shall see his Saviour face to face.

He will come, as He promised; and it may be soon.

G. T. MANLEY

THE PROMISE

AMID all that is hard to understand in the prophecies of
the Bible there is one prediction which stands out clear
and certain, namely the promise that the Lord Jesus
Christ will come again. It is obviously of supreme importance
that we should understand the bearing of this fact upon our
own lives. Leaving aside for the moment, therefore, the doubts
and difficulties, let us face the essential question: *Is* He really
coming again?

An illustration may help us. An artist has depicted a young
woman standing on a cliff, looking out to sea, her hand
shading her eyes, as she scans the horizon for the first sign of
her husband's returning ship. And why does she look so
eagerly, with such evident and intense desire? It is because she
trusts his word about the time of his return, and because she
loves him, and his presence means more to her than all the
world beside. For this reason she will recall exactly what he
said when he promised to return, and especially what he told
her about the time when she might expect to see him; she will
look for some sign of the approach of his ship; she will prepare
for him the welcome which is always ready in her heart.

Even so will the Christian, who loves his Saviour and looks
for His appearing, study every word of promise laid up in the
Scriptures and scan the political horizon for any sign that the
time of its fulfilment is drawing near. To be sure there are
differences between the Lord's coming and that of an earthly
companion; but there are also parallels, and chief among these
is the fact that He gave a definite assurance that He would
indeed return.

It is the purpose of this chapter to consider first His own
words as given in the Gospels, and then to study their confirmation in the Acts and the Epistles.

ON THE MOUNT OF OLIVES

We will begin with the Gospel of Mark. Whilst ourselves believing in the full inspiration of all Scripture, it is not necessary for us here to assume more than that upon which competent scholars of most schools of thought all agree, namely, that here we have an honest record. According to Papias, who wrote early in the second century and had known some of the apostles, and elders contemporary with them, Mark was the 'interpreter' of Peter and wrote down 'accurately' what he heard from Peter himself. His Gospel contains three sayings of Christ which refer to His return; on two of these occasions Peter was present, and on the third he was near at hand.

The first of these occurred in circumstances which must have stamped themselves on Peter's mind (see Mk. viii. 27–38). His bold declaration of faith, 'Thou art the Christ', his impetuous rebuke of his Master and the way in which Jesus 'turned' to rebuke *him*,[1] are all graphically told. Then Jesus called the others to listen and said, 'Whosoever will come after me, let him deny himself, and take up his cross, and follow me.' Finally He added, 'Whosoever therefore shall be ashamed of me and of my words in this adulterous and sinful generation; of him also shall the Son of man be ashamed, when he cometh in the glory of his Father with the holy angels.'

The second occasion was two days after His triumphal entry into Jerusalem. Jesus had with Him Peter and Andrew, and James and John, and as they left the temple, and were remarking on its glories, He predicted its destruction. They were on their way to Bethany, and as they ascended the Mount of Olives, and rested for a while at a spot overlooking the city, the disciples asked, 'When shall these things be? and what shall be the sign when all these things shall be fulfilled?' (Mk. xiii. 4). The form of the question implies that He had been speaking of some of the things which are referred to in His reply. How

---

[1] This detail is peculiar to Mark, a significant sign of its Petrine origin.

we wish we could have been with them, listening to the words of our common Master! That cannot be; but we may be grateful for the recording of them, and may study them with care. Their vivid and pictorial character, in the true spirit of Hebrew prophecy, is an attestation, if any were needed, of their genuineness.

The reply falls naturally into three sections. In the first of these (verses 5–13) He forewarns them of trials through which they will have to pass when He will no longer be with them, though the Holy Spirit will teach them how to answer. In the second (verses 14–23) He foresees coming in the siege of Jerusalem a time of unprecedented 'tribulation' (rv), such as was foretold by Daniel (Dn. xii. 1), from which, however, some will be able to escape. Here there is a break, and He resumes, 'But in those days, after that tribulation, the sun shall be darkened, and the moon shall not give her light, and the stars of heaven shall fall, and the powers that are in heaven shall be shaken' (Mk. xiii. 24, 25). The words are reminiscent of what Joel and Isaiah had said would come to pass afterward in the day of the Lord (Joel ii. 28ff.; Is. xiii. 9, 20). He then proceeds, 'And then shall they see the Son of man coming in the clouds with great power and glory. And then shall he send his angels, and shall gather together his elect from the four winds, from the uttermost part of the earth to the uttermost part of heaven' (Mk. xiii. 26, 27). There can be no mistaking the meaning; at some future time man will see Him coming.

The third occasion was when Jesus was brought before the high priest (Mk. xiv. 53), who challenged Him with the words, 'Art thou the Christ, the Son of the Blessed?' He receives the reply, 'I am: and ye shall see the Son of man sitting on the right hand of power, and coming in the clouds of heaven' (Mk. xiv. 61, 62; cf. Dn. vii. 13).[1] The message is the same.

---

[1] On the word 'henceforth' in the parallel passage in Matthew (xxvi. 64, rv), see N. B. Stonehouse, *The Witness of Matthew and Mark to Christ* (Tyndale Press, 1959), pp. 240 ff.

THE TESTIMONY OF PETER

Peter's own witness is first found in the Acts of the Apostles, in the first twelve chapters of which he appears as the central figure. He had seen the risen Lord on more than one occasion during the forty days between His resurrection and ascension. He had heard His parting words, had gazed in wonder as He was taken up and a cloud received Him out of their sight, and had heard the words of the men who announced His return. With his companions, he had then returned to Jerusalem and the upper room, where those present are mentioned by name (Acts i. 8–13).

In those days he addressed a gathering numbering about a hundred on the need of replacing Judas Iscariot by one who had companied with them from the baptism of John up to the time of the ascension. The story of the ascension, whether originating from Peter or one of his companions, is simply and honestly told and bears the evidence of truth upon its face. The time and place are specified, all eleven were witnesses, their return to Jerusalem follows and then these humble toilers of the despised province of Galilee betook themselves to prayer.

On the day of Pentecost Peter declares that Jesus has been exalted to God's right hand, there to reign till His enemies be made His footstool (Acts ii. 33, 35). Again, after healing a man lame from birth, he addresses his astonished hearers, calls upon them to repent, and says that God 'shall send Jesus Christ, which before was preached unto you: whom the heaven must receive until the times of restitution of all things' (Acts iii. 20, 21).

Whether it be 'this same Jesus' coming, or God sending Him, Peter looks forward to His certain return, though at a time unknown.

What is told us in Acts is confirmed in Peter's two Epistles. In the former of these he addresses those who love the Lord Jesus though they have not seen Him (1 Pet. i. 8). They are being kept by faith, he says, 'unto salvation ready to be revealed in the last time' (1 Pet. i. 5); therefore he exhorts them to 'hope to the end for the grace that is to be brought unto you at the revelation of Jesus Christ' (1 Pet. i. 13). Later on he writes, 'the end of all things is at hand: be ye therefore sober, and watch unto prayer' (1 Pet. iv. 7), words which seem reminiscent of those of Jesus, 'watch and pray: for ye know not when the time is' (Mk. xiii. 33).

In his second letter he deals at some length with the words of certain scoffers, who had arisen, saying, 'Where is the promise of his coming (Gk., *parousia*)?' (2 Pet. iii. 4). The question shows that the expectation of His return was widespread in the community. In reply Peter affirms that 'the Lord is not slack concerning his promise . . . ; but is longsuffering to us-ward, not willing that any should perish, but that all should come to repentance'. Nevertheless 'the day of the Lord will come as a thief in the night' (2 Pet. iii. 9, 10). The metaphor is one derived from a saying of Jesus inculcating faithful service (Lk. xii. 39) which had already attained currency among the disciples. Here is a long chain of evidence, with many undesigned coincidences, that Peter maintained this hope throughout his life.

The Olivet discourse is also reported in the Gospels of Matthew and Luke with some small variations and some valuable additions. They reproduce the identical words 'they shall see the Son of man coming'; Matthew adds 'in the clouds of heaven with power and great glory' (Mt. xxiv. 30; cf. Lk. xxi. 27). The relationship of the first three, or synoptic, Gospels is a problem of some complexity.[1] Both Papias and Irenaeus independently tell us that Matthew collected the Lord's sayings in the original Hebrew; and there is reason to believe that the first committing of them to writing was not long after they were spoken. The reports in these Gospels therefore confirm that we have here a genuine saying of the Lord.

[1] See a small, but valuable, book by Professor F. F. Bruce, *The New Testament Documents: Are They Reliable?* (I.V.F.).

THE WITNESS OF JOHN

We now turn to the witness of John, who was also in the group that questioned the Lord on the Mount of Olives, saw Him during the forty days after His resurrection, and was present when He ascended into heaven. In chapters xiii to xvi of his Gospel he records teaching given by the Lord after the Passover meal. Jesus repeats words He had spoken to the Jews, 'Whither I go, ye cannot come' (Jn. xiii. 33; cf. viii. 21).[1] Peter protests, and is told that he will deny his Master. Their hearts are troubled, but Jesus encourages them, and so encourages us, to believe in Himself. He also reassures them: 'I go to prepare a place for you. And if I go and prepare a place for you, I will come again, and receive you unto myself; that where I am, there ye may be also' (Jn. xiv. 2, 3).[2] The words puzzled them; but the central promise is clear, 'I will come again'.

'His "coming" would begin with His resurrection, but not end there. His "presence" (*parousia*) is distinctly implied here' (Westcott). There are some who see in the words 'I will come again' nothing more than a reference to the gift of the Spirit at Pentecost. There is, of course, a sense in which Jesus 'came' to His disciples then, as He 'comes' today to those who receive Him into their hearts. But that is not the meaning here. No plainer words could be found to express a quite literal departure and return; He goes to His Father's house to prepare a 'place'; He will come again to gather the believers round Him.

His words concerning the gift of the Comforter are quite different, and the two should not be confused. He tells them that in answer to His prayer, the Father will 'send' the Comforter, and 'he dwelleth with you, and shall be in you' (Jn. xiv. 16, 17, 26). The disciples certainly did not confuse the two promises; both in the Acts and the Epistles Pentecost is

[1] The Greek word *hupagein* is one in common use meaning 'to go', 'to go away', 'to depart'.
[2] Here the Greek has *poreuesthai*, another common word meaning 'to go' or 'to take a journey'; cf. Acts ix. 3.

plainly a past event, whilst the *parousia*[1] is looked for in the future.

In the last chapter of his Gospel, John describes how, after His resurrection, Jesus showed Himself to a group of disciples, of whom he was one (xxi. 1, 2), by the sea of Tiberias. Jesus eats with them, and then draws from Peter a threefold declaration of his love, after which Jesus forecasts the manner of death by which Peter should glorify God. Seeing John following, Peter enquires, 'Lord, and what shall this man do?' Jesus answers, 'If I will that he tarry till I come, what is that to thee? follow thou me' (Jn. xxi. 21, 22). The closing verses reveal that the account of these words obtained a wide circulation and gave rise to a belief that John would not die, which the writer[2] corrects. It is a wonderful story, but known to be true (verse 24), and it clearly points to John's expectation that Jesus will really come again.

In his first Epistle, John looks forward to the time when Jesus will appear, when 'we shall see him as he is' (1 Jn. iii. 2). Finally, in the book of Revelation, which we believe to be also his work, we have once again the words, 'Behold, he cometh with clouds; and every eye shall see him' (Rev. i. 7).

As we recall that Peter and John were both members of the little group on the Mount of Olives, the recurrence in their writings of the very words in which He there made the announcement of His return, serves to render our assurance doubly sure.

THE EXPECTATION OF THE EARLY CHURCH

We have been concentrating attention upon the witness of Peter and John because of the value it acquires owing to their close companionship with Jesus Himself. Even if it stood alone, it would suffice to assure us that we may look forward to His coming, and possibly live to see it. But this testimony

---

[1] For the meaning of this word see below, p. 16.
[2] Probably John himself, though some regard these verses as a later addition.

does not stand alone; the New Testament is full of references to Christ's return, more or less direct, and they offer a wide and highly interesting field for study, as we shall see. They are to be found in every one of the twenty-seven books of the New Testament, except the Epistle to the Galatians (which had a special object) and the short Epistles, Philemon and 2 and 3 John.

The personal character of the Advent to which the early disciples were looking forward is shown by the Greek word most frequently used for it, namely, the *parousia*. In secular Greek this was the word used for the visit of an emperor or other distinguished person. A literal translation would be 'being nearby', so that it combines the notions of 'approach' and 'presence', with a suggestion of honour due to the person to whom it refers. It is well illustrated in 2 Corinthians vii. 6, 7 where Paul describes the pleasure which the advent, or 'coming', of Titus afforded him. The same thought is present when he writes of the 'coming' of Stephanas and his companions (1 Cor. xvi. 17) or his own 'coming' to Philippi (Phil. i. 26), both happy events.

In reference to the Advent of Jesus Christ the word is used seven times by Paul,[1] twice by James,[2] three times by Peter,[3] and once by John.[4] It is also found four times in Matthew's account of the Olivet discourse;[5] but all we can deduce from this is that this word was in common use when the Greek version of Matthew came to be made. In every case the word is used for the coming of a person, or group of persons. In the second century it was used in isolation to mean the Advent of Jesus Christ.

Another word, *epiphaneia*, used only by Paul,[6] is of a more general character, and means 'appearing'. Paul also uses this of the first coming of Jesus Christ into the world (2 Tim. i. 10),

---

[1] 1 Cor. xv. 23; 1 Thes. ii. 19, iii. 13, iv. 15, v. 23; 2 Thes. ii. 1, 8.
[2] Jas. v. 7, 8.   [3] 2 Pet. i. 16, iii. 4, 12.   [4] 1 Jn. ii. 28.
[5] Mt. xxiv. 3, 27, 37, 39.
[6] 2 Thes. ii. 8 (AV, 'brightness'); 1 Tim. vi. 14; 2 Tim. iv. 1, 8; Tit. ii. 13.

an unquestionably historical event. It is appropriate in reference to meeting once again with someone already known.

The Advent is also described as the 'revelation' (*apokalupsis*) of Jesus Christ.[1] Here again the references show that it is regarded as an event in the future. The writer to the Hebrews says that He 'shall be seen' by those who look for Him (ix. 28). Taking these various expressions together we get a clear picture of the Advent, seen through the eyes of the early Church. It would mean His presence after His absence, the shining of His glory after His humiliation, and the unveiling of His majesty and power.

In addition to these references we have Paul's word about the Lord's Supper, that in it the Lord's death is declared 'till he come' (1 Cor. xi. 26).

In the book of Revelation, as we have already noted, the expectation of a visible return of Christ is perfectly definite. 'Behold, he cometh with clouds; and every eye shall see him' (Rev. i. 7). 'Behold,' John cries, 'He is coming,' as if with the eye of faith he could see Him already on His way.

This, then, was the attitude of the early Church, and should be ours today. Let us look back with deep thanksgiving upon the cross where He bore our sins; let us look up to the heavens where He is seated on the right hand of God, ever making intercession for us; and let us look forward to His coming again. According to the teaching of the New Testament, 'that return is an event, not a process; and is personal and corporeal.'[2]

There is one more expression, frequently misunderstood, with which we may bring this brief review of the New Testament outlook on the Advent to a close. At the end of Paul's first letter to the Corinthians, after sending greetings to his friends and putting his signature to the salutation, he adds, 'If any man loveth not the Lord, let him be anathema. Maran atha' (1 Cor. xvi. 22, RV). 'Anathema' is a Greek word meaning 'set aside' or 'put away', often for a special use, such as a votive offering. 'Maran atha' are two Aramaic words meaning 'Our

[1] 1 Cor. i. 7 (RV); 2 Thes. i. 7; 1 Pet. i. 7 (RV), 13.
[2] Note on Acts i. 11 in the 'Scofield Bible'.

Lord cometh'.[1] Their introduction into a letter, written in Greek, without any explanation, shows that they were in current use, and would be understood by Paul's readers, many of them of Gentile origin. That this was actually the case is confirmed by the appearing of these two words in early Christian writings such as the *Didache*, where a form of thanksgiving is given to be used after the Lord's Supper which ends, 'Maran atha, Amen'. It seems to have been a common greeting within the Christian fellowship. Paul uses a Greek equivalent in Philippians iv. 5. This explains 1 Corinthians xvi. 22. It is as if Paul says: 'The Lord is coming. Do you love Him? If not, the Christian fellowship is no place for you.'

THE CREED

As the Church grew and spread, it was felt that more should be required of candidates for baptism than the simple affirmation 'Jesus is Lord' (1 Cor. xii. 3), namely that they should assent to certain fundamental beliefs. These should include not only belief in God the Father, in Jesus Christ and in the Holy Spirit, but in the central facts of the life of Jesus, the Son of God.

At the end of the second century, a creed of Tertullian in his *de Virginibus Velendis* included the words, 'Sitting now at the right hand of the Father, will come to judge the quick and the dead.' Augustine's sermons show that these articles were in the Creed which he taught his candidates for baptism.

But is it really true? For there are those who deny it. But to us the evidence which we have advanced seems to prove beyond a doubt that Jesus promised to return; and for us His word is final. And if it be true, is it not exciting and tremendously important to think that you may live to see Him come again? What a host of problems and questions it raises! How and when could it happen? It is often remarked that events in the world seem to be moving to a climax; could it

---

[1] Or, 'has come'. See further L. Morris, *Commentary on 1 Corinthians*, (Tyndale Press, 1958), pp. 247f.

be, then, that the promise could be fulfilled, say within the next five years? Does the Bible tell us of signs which will show whether the return of Christ is near? There is also the more searching question, Am I ready to meet Him?

These questions should be faced, and that without delay, for 'ye know neither the day nor the hour' (Mt. xxv. 13).

It is the object of this book to help the reader to find an answer to these questions, and to clear away some of the difficulties. In our next chapter we shall take the Lord as our Teacher, and seek to learn, and apply to the present day, some of the lessons contained in the Olivet discourse to which reference has already been made.

CHAPTER II

TEACHING FOR TODAY

SOME PERSONAL TESTIMONIES

THE reader who has got thus far will easily agree that the subject is important and will repay study; but he may not be convinced that it is practical or requires immediate attention. The young man embarking on his career or the student with exams looming ahead may be disposed to put off further consideration of it to a more convenient season. Before deciding this let them reflect how important a place it occupies in the teaching of Christ and in the New Testament generally, and how vital an influence it has exercised upon the lives of many people, great and humble. Some testimonies will be of interest. They are purposely drawn from widely differing times and circumstances.

Lord Shaftesbury, who introduced so many beneficial reforms into our social system, said towards the end of his life, 'I do not think that in the last forty years I have lived one conscious hour that was not influenced by the thought of our Lord's return.' How it affected the life of a lady who, for her own day, had a very modern outlook indeed, can be read in Christabel Pankhurst's book, *The Lord Cometh*. She had made a name for herself by her vigorous part in the campaign for votes for women. Writing in 1923 she said: 'By what seemed a chance discovery in a bookshop, I came across writings on prophecy which pointed out that in the Bible there are oracles foretelling and diagnosing the world's ills, and promising that they should be cured.' This was to be brought about, not by political agitation, but by the Lord's return. 'It seemed too good to be true,' she writes. This changed the course of her life, and this brilliant young law student gave herself up to lecturing in public on the return of Christ as foretold in the Scriptures.

Or take an example of a quite different kind. In a recent review (1959) of C.M.S. policy in East Africa these words occur: 'The Society believes in the Coming Great Church, one day to be consummated by the appearing of Christ in His glory, and to this end actively participates in all progress towards united action by different denominations and in plans for the organic union of churches.'

One more example; a young man, converted less than a year, told a friend of the writer, 'The Second Advent colours my whole life; everything is affected by it. The Lord will come suddenly, and I must be ready.'

Such testimonies show how social reform, political action, church reunion and the individual life, all receive strength and impetus from the hope of the Lord's return.

As we proceed we shall find abundant evidence of how practical was the influence of the doctrine on the lives of the first believers. But for the present chapter we shall limit our attention to a closer study of Jesus' Olivet discourse. We shall observe how He there diverted the disciples' thought from curious questioning to helpful practical teaching. We shall find that it contains personal exhortations of great and immediate value to ourselves. As we study afresh His words, let us not forget that, however applicable they are to ourselves, we are dealing with the record of an actual conversation once addressed to four disciples whose names are given, and we must interpret the words in consonance with the circumstances in which they were spoken. As we read between the lines, we can see how the Lord loved them too well to buoy them up with false hopes, but, as often before, was training them for the vital part which they would play in the establishment of the kingdom of God.

He begins by warning them of the opposition and false rumours which they would soon encounter; and then predicts in general terms the terrors of the siege which Jerusalem would undergo, a type of the persecution which Christians would experience until the time of His return in glory. It should be observed that Jesus does not give a direct answer to their question, When? Instead, He gives them useful counsel for the immediate and more distant future. As Professor Swete says in his commentary, 'The tone of the prediction is wholly practical.' He gave them the teaching they needed for the coming days, He forewarned them of the dangers, encouraged them to endure, and inspired them by the prospect of His coming. He is the same today, and deals with our questionings in like manner. We would often like to know our future, what will happen to us next year, or it may be next week. We go to the Scriptures, and what we read there is what *He* wishes us to know, teaching for today.

The words must have made a deep impression: they are recorded by the first three evangelists, and each has something of his own to contribute. They remember the exact place and His very posture (Mk. xiii. 3); the names of the four listeners and the questions they asked (verse 4; cf. Mt. xxiv. 3). He answered them with sympathetic understanding, preparing them to meet the trials and testings which awaited them. His predictions dealt with the fall of Jerusalem, but carried on far beyond, even to the end of the age. They are as vivid today as on the day they were spoken; let us listen to them with hearts determined loyally to obey whatever concerns ourselves.

DIVINE IMPERATIVES

The discourse is punctuated with a series of *imperatives*, of which the first is 'Take heed . . .'. Let us obey this straightway and consider the others in order, as they occur in Mark xiii. 'Take heed' (5). 'Be ye not troubled' (7). 'Take heed to yourselves' (9). 'Take no thought beforehand' (11). 'Flee to the mountains' (14). 'Believe him not' (21). 'Take ye heed' (23). 'Learn a parable' (28). 'Take ye heed, watch and pray' (33). 'Watch' (35). 'Watch' (37). Luke adds another: 'Look up, and lift up your heads; for . . .' (Lk. xxi. 28). As we glance down the list it is easy to see that this is exactly the kind of warning and encouragement these four disciples needed. But were they meant for them alone? This may be the case with the advice to flee to the mountains when they saw the temple profaned; but what of the rest? They deal with (a) dangers to avoid, (b) encouragement to persevere, (c) work to be done, (d) an alert and watchful attitude, and best of all, (e) the incentive of a glorious hope.

a. Dangers to avoid

The Lord's first words are 'Take heed' and these He repeats another three times (verses 5, 9, 23, 33). Surely here is something most important. He gives His reasons each time, and the first is 'lest any man deceive you'. He knew that many impostors would arise; Bar-cochba in those days, Mahomet later, and others who have a following today. A second danger, no less serious, is lest faith fail in face of opposition and persecution. Peter fell through heedlessness, and many another has done since. A third danger arises from 'false prophets'; they may be very intellectual, and be so clever as 'to seduce, if it were possible, even the elect' (Mk. xiii. 22). But the Christian need not be deceived, if he obey the command that follows, 'Take ye heed: behold, I have foretold you all things.'

When Paul was on his way to Jerusalem and the elders came from Ephesus to Miletus to greet him, he warned them of this same danger, that grievous wolves would enter the fold, teaching perverse things, and repeated the words 'Take heed' (Acts xx. 28–31). How serious the danger was can be seen from the strong language used in the letters to the seven churches (Rev. ii. 2, 9, 20) or in Paul's letter to Timothy (1 Tim. iv. 1–3). The danger will not grow less, 'evil men and seducers shall wax worse and worse, deceiving, and being deceived' (2 Tim. iii. 13).

Finally, Jesus tells His disciples, 'Take ye heed' for 'ye know not when the time is' (Mk. xiii. 33). Will the reader, before he passes on, ask himself whether he is taking due heed in these four directions?

b. Encouragement to endure

'When ye shall hear of wars and rumours of wars, be ye not troubled.' These words strengthened the faith and confidence of those who first heard them; and many living today who have passed through either one or two world wars have experienced their staying power. A correspondent to a religious journal recently wrote, 'In a day when material things can be blown to bits in seconds and the dimensions of time and space have lost much of their significance, there is a hunger on the part of people for spiritual values which sustain in times of crisis.'[1] As for 'rumours of wars', is not the air thick with them? One opens a daily paper and reads, 'A month ago we were on the very edge, on the very brink, of a world war.'[2]

Jesus foresaw these things and assured His followers. Was there ever a teacher so practical and so helpful? Even though the threat of a still more fearful war hangs over our heads, 'be not troubled', for beyond is the time when our Jesus will be seen coming in power and glory. We have no need to fear. Once again He encouraged them to endure persecution. 'When they shall lead you, and deliver you up, take no thought beforehand what ye shall speak . . .' for the Holy Spirit would teach them what to say. Not long after, Peter was set before the high priest, and found the promise literally fulfilled (Acts iv. 1-13).

It is still available, and one upon which we can rely. Upon it Christians in communist China are resting. One in close touch with events there writes, 'The only rift in a black sky is the promise of the coming of the Lord.'[3]

c. Work to do

In answer to their question, When? the Lord points them to an immediate duty. 'The gospel must first be published among all nations.' Good news, and for everybody; this must be proclaimed first; this is a *primary* duty. Again on the Mount of Olives, on the day of ascension, they asked whether the time had come to restore the kingdom to Israel; and again He brushes aside the matter of 'the times and the seasons' and

---

[1] *Christianity Today*, July 1958.
[2] *Yorkshire Post*, 12th August, 1958.
[3] *The Millions*, October 1958.

promises them power that they may be His witnesses 'unto the uttermost part of the earth'. These are His last recorded words on earth, and the last from heaven are, 'Surely I come quickly' (Rev. xxii. 20).

Is there any connection between them? They were taken seriously then, and form the keynote of the Acts of the Apostles; but when the persecutions ended, and the Church was popular and at ease, they fell into oblivion.

In the closing years of the nineteenth century a movement arose in the universities which took shape in Britain as the Student Volunteer Missionary Union. In January 1896 a conference of members was held at Liverpool, at which its leaders announced the adoption of the watchword, 'The Evangelization of the World in this Generation'. Some, but not all, looked upon this as the dream of enthusiastic young men. But Archbishop Frederick Temple welcomed it and passed it on to the Lambeth Conference of 1897 for consideration. It was in fact, even then, an ideal within the powers of professing Christians to accomplish, if only they had bent themselves to the task. Instead it remained an ideal and inspiration for the few, and thirty years later large regions of the world remained unevangelized. Then a new generation of student volunteers arose who adopted the cry, 'Evangelize to a finish, to bring back the King.'

The imperative of Matthew xxviii. 19, 'Go ye therefore, and teach all nations', still remains, and is incumbent upon us, even though Christian churches of considerable size in Africa, India and the Far East are today all sharing in the task of publishing the good news.

d. Watch and pray

In Mark xiii. Jesus laid upon them another duty. Like the command to take heed, it is emphasized by reiteration; 'watch and pray' (33); 'watch ye therefore; for ye know not when' (35); 'what I say unto you I say unto all, Watch' (37). On this last saying Theophylact's comment is, 'The Lord announces this to all, to the man of the world as well as to the recluse', and we might add, to the Christians of the twentieth century as well as to those of the first.

How immediately they needed it! Two days later, in the garden of Gethsemane, the words are repeated to Peter and James and John, 'Watch ye and pray, lest ye enter into temptation' (Mk. xiv. 38). But they fell asleep; and there are sleeping Christians today. Peter probably had the Lord's words in mind when he wrote, 'the end of all things is at hand: be ye therefore sober, and watch unto prayer' (1 Pet. iv. 7). To watch is an active duty, to be like the sentry on the look-out to see what or who is coming. It is especially appropriate in connection with the watching for the coming of the Lord. For such watching, Paul has a very expressive word, *apek-dechomai*, 'looking eagerly', or literally 'stretching out away', as if anxious to be the first to give Him a welcome (see 1 Cor. i. 7; Phil. iii. 20; cf. Heb. ix. 28). Such indeed we need to be as the time draws nearer.

In Matthew's account the command to watch is emphasized by the simile of the householder who would have watched had he known when the thief would come (Mt. xxiv. 42ff.). It is again repeated as the moral of the parable of the ten virgins (xxv. 13). It is perhaps only a variation of the command to watch which we have in Matthew xxiv. 44, 'Therefore be ye also ready: for in such an hour as ye think not the Son of man cometh.' 'Ready' is repeated in the ensuing parable, where the wise virgins are described as 'they that were ready' (Mt. xxv. 10). Their lamps were burning, and they had a supply of oil; a picture of the Christian whose life shines before men because of the inward illumination of the Holy Spirit. Such will welcome the Bridegroom with joy when He appears.

We may well ask ourselves, am I thus ready? There is yet time; the supply of the Spirit is not limited, nor for sale. Shall not your heavenly Father 'give the Holy Spirit to them that ask him'? (Lk. xi. 13). We might find another imperative in the words, 'Now learn a parable of the fig tree' (Mk. xiii. 28), which adds to the need for watchfulness and an intelligent outlook upon current events and their consequences. One friend sees a sign of the end of this age in the rising tide of nationalism, another in the increase of Russian power, another in the progress of the Israel state. They may be right or not, but the duty to observe 'the signs of the times' and to try to interpret them in the light of Scripture is plain enough; that is the parable of the fig tree.

e. The needed incentive: a glorious prospect

'Then look up, and lift up your heads,' the Lord said. When? 'When these things begin to come to pass'; and He had just spoken of great convulsions and of 'men's hearts failing them for fear, and for looking after those things which are coming on the earth' (Lk. xxi. 26, 28). These things have begun to come to pass; the words could have been spoken yesterday. And why should we look up? Because 'your redemption draweth nigh' (Lk. xxi. 28); and our redemption is concentrated in the Person of our Redeemer. Let the pessimist look down, and the fearful look around; but let the Christian lift up his head and look up.

There can be no greater cause of encouragement and hope for the Christian than the expectation of meeting his Redeemer. Here is, and always has been, an 'incentive to enterprise' greater than any money rewards. 'Wherefore gird up the loins of your mind, be sober, and hope to the end for the grace that is to be brought unto you at the revelation of Jesus Christ' (1 Pet. i. 13).

PRECEPT AND PRACTICE

The New Testament contains clear evidence as to the way in which these precepts coloured the thoughts and affected the conduct of the first generation of Christians. Most of the references to the Advent in the Epistles are accompanied by some practical application. Very notable was the way in which, when they were persecuted, they went everywhere preaching the word (Acts viii. 4). There was little need to send missionaries; they were all missionaries. Besides what we are told in the Acts of the Apostles, Peter travelled to Egypt (1 Pet. v. 13)[1] and later to Rome, and tradition says that Thomas founded the Church in India, and James carried the gospel to Spain.

Some examples have been given, and more could be added, of echoes in the Epistles of the Lord's exhortations to take heed, to watch and to be ready, and of His likening His coming at a time unexpected to that of a thief in the night. The thought of the Advent is also connected with, and a stimulus to, strivings after holiness, that the converts may be found 'unblameable in holiness' (1 Thes. iii. 13; cf. Col. iii. 1, 2).[2] Combined with this is the looking for a perfected redemption and full salvation brought about through His actual presence (1 Pet. i. 5; Heb. ix. 28). Let anyone read through at one sitting the two Epistles to the Thessalonians and he cannot fail to be struck with the way that every part of the teaching leads up to, and is dominated by, the prospect of the Lord's return.

It is a hope, a 'lively' hope (1 Pet. i. 3), a 'blessed' hope (Tit. ii. 13), a hope that leads to purity of life (1 Jn. iii. 3). Is this not exactly what we need today, to raise our standards and to invigorate our zeal?

---

[1] 'Babylon' is, probably, as an early Coptic tradition asserts, the Roman colony on the Nile, where the remains of the fort can still be seen in Old Cairo. The name still lingers as Babloun. See the writer's article in *The Evangelical Quarterly* for April 1944, pp. 138–146.

[2] See also below, p. 97.

CHAPTER III

WHEN?

THE four disciples put to Jesus their question 'when shall these things be?' (Mk. xiii. 4), and the same question has been asked by Christians ever since. But, as we have seen, Jesus' answer began, 'Take heed lest any man deceive you.' He warned them of trials, and gave them signs connected with them; He announced His coming, but for that He gave no date. On the contrary His answer was, 'But of that day and that hour knoweth no man' (Mk. xiii. 32). Let us then confess frankly that we do not know when. On the eve of the ascension the disciples put another question, 'Wilt thou at this time restore again the kingdom to Israel?' To which He answered, 'It is not for you to know the times or the seasons, which the Father hath put in his own power' (Acts i. 6, 7). Perhaps we are not meant to know the time.

But is this all that can be said? By no means! There have been many scholars of ability and devotion who have believed that certain mystic figures in the books of Daniel and Revelation could be interpreted upon the year-day principle to indicate the approaching end of the age. In their view these figures were only to be understood in the latter days, when by their means an approximate date of the Advent could be fixed, whilst still leaving open 'the day and the hour'. It was thought by some that a connection existed between 'the times of the Gentiles' (Lk. xxi. 24) and the 'seven times' in Daniel iv. 16, 25, 32. Since elsewhere a 'time' is the equivalent of a year,[1] this was taken to represent 2,520 (7 × 360) years. If the starting-point be taken as the time when Jerusalem came under the sovereignty of Nebuchadnezzar this indicated a time early in the twentieth century for the end of the age.

[1] Cf. Rev. xii. 6 and 14.

When the World War broke out in 1914 in all its fierceness, the question was raised, even in the secular press, Is this Armageddon?[1] There seemed to be further confirmation for these ideas when in 1917 Jerusalem was delivered from the power of the Turk, and the Balfour declaration promised a 'national home' for the Jews in Palestine. In 1918 a book appeared by C. I. Scofield, in which he wrote that the words in Luke xxi. 24 'obviously refer to the political role of the Gentiles. . . . With the conquest of Jerusalem by Nebuchad-nezzar, 606 BC, began the period of more than 2,500 years' duration in which we are living, and of which the present world war may be the beginning of the end.' The world did not come to an end then, and in 1939 there started the Second World War. The following year B. F. C. Atkinson published a book, *The War with Satan*, in which the same figure, 2,520, was used, in conjunction with others, to show that the time was running out.

We may be grateful to these and other writers for focusing attention on the Scriptures which relate to the latter days and keeping alive the expectation of the Lord's return; but it is clear that caution is needed in the exact interpretation of numbers. And if scholars of repute have been mistaken, less responsible writers have fallen into more serious error.

IN MY LIFETIME?

If then the Advent be near, it is natural to wonder whether we ourselves shall live to see the Lord coming in the clouds. It seems probable that many now living will do so. This seems to have been Peter's expectation when he told the people that God 'shall send Jesus Christ, which before was preached unto you: whom the heaven must receive until the times of restitution of all things' (Acts iii. 20f.). The same is seen, though as a hope rather than as an assurance, in his first Epistle, where he writes, 'be sober, and hope to the end for the grace that is to be brought unto you at the revelation of

[1] *What do the Prophets Say?*, Marshall, p. 10.

Jesus Christ' (1 Pet. i. 13, and cf. i. 7, iv. 7). His second Epistle shows that the question was being much discussed at that time by believers and by 'scoffers' (2 Pet. iii. 3–11). He gives reasons for the delay and exhorts his readers to 'holy living and godliness'; let them be looking for and hastening the day of God. His attitude is one of expectation and hope, but not of assertion or certainty as regards the time. But the event itself is certain.

A careful reading of John xxi reveals the same outlook on the part of St. John. The coming of the Lord had been discussed among the disciples, and some had understood the words which the Lord addressed to Peter to mean that John would never see death. John attempts no prophecy, and is content to note that the Lord did not assert this, but only '*If* I will that he tarry till I come, what is that to thee?' (Jn. xxi. 23).

The testimony of Peter and John is important for the interpretation of the Lord's own words, since they were both among His listeners on the Mount of Olives. They were not deceived as to the time; Jesus had told them that it was not known to men, and they trusted His word. Certain critics have read the words of Jesus in Mark xiii. 30 as a prediction that He would return within a generation, and have concluded that He was mistaken. But this interpretation of the words cannot be sustained.

When the disciples asked, 'When shall these things be?' (Mk. xiii. 4), 'these things' can refer only to that which immediately precedes, namely, the destruction of the temple, and whatever else He said in that connection. His answer, as already noted, falls into three sections, of which the first consists of warnings regarding the immediate future, the second deals with the siege of Jerusalem, and the third briefly announces that at some future time men will see Him coming with clouds. Then, after bidding them learn a parable of the fig tree, He adds, 'Verily I say unto you, that this generation shall not pass (*parelthē*,) till all these things be done' (Mk. xiii. 30). There is a double ambiguity, both as to the meaning of 'these things' and as to that of the word 'generation'. The words 'all these things' repeat those of the original question, and therefore could be taken as referring back to that only. Again, the word *genea*, 'generation', can mean either a 'race' or a 'length of time'. Jerome, commenting on this verse, took it in the former sense, 'the human, or especially the Jewish race'. But the meaning could quite well be, 'the troubles of which I have been telling you, will all come to pass in this generation of time'.

To accuse the Lord of misleading the disciples about the time of His return is absurd[1] seeing that He expressly said that He did not know it! His words have been pressed into use to support the Kenosis theory, and to show that His teaching was not free from error. But read them again, for they are very striking. 'But of that day or that hour knoweth no one, not even the angels in heaven, neither the Son, but the Father' (Mk. xiii. 32, RV). This approaches to a claim to divinity, rather than the contrary; for He places Himself above the angels and next to God the Father. The implication is that they would expect Him to know, but that for some special reason He did not. He knew that the temple would be destroyed and Jerusalem besieged, but this was hidden from Him. The reason is not far to seek. There are certain times and seasons which God retains in His own power (Acts i. 7); and it was part of His plan that the hope of the Saviour's return should shine as a light to lead on and encourage one generation after another. As Jesus was tempted but did not sin, so He accepted human limitations, but did not err.

The Pauline Epistles show the same attitude in the early Church; these first Christians were looking for the coming of Jesus Christ but were aware that the time could not be foretold. In the Lord's Supper they proclaimed His death 'till he come' (1 Cor. xi. 26), but they did not know when that would be. The view of many modern scholars, that in early life Paul entertained the hope of living to see this return, but that he

[1] See N. B. Stonehouse, *The Witness of Matthew and Mark to Christ* (Tyndale Press, 1959), pp. 238–240.

changed his ideas both as to the time and manner of His coming, is one which must be rejected on a fair reading of the evidence. It is true that the words 'we which are alive and remain' in 1 Thessalonians iv. 15 suggest that he hoped to be among them; but it is no less true that the words which follow in 1 Thessalonians v. 2 suggest uncertainty, while those in 2 Thessalonians ii speak of delay. His letter to the Galatians, which was among the earliest, perhaps the first of all, does not mention the *parousia*; and its prominence in 1 Thessalonians is due in part to the circumstances (1 Thes. iv. 14, 18). Years afterwards, when he wrote the Epistle to the Philippians, he was still looking for the Lord to come (Phil. iv. 5; see also p. 18). It was only natural that when he wrote the Second Epistle to Timothy, with the prospect of an almost immediate death sentence before him, he should no longer think of *himself* as experiencing the *parousia*; but nevertheless he still thinks of his fellow Christians as those who love the Lord's 'appearing' (2 Tim. iv. 6–8).

The same outlook is given expression in the Epistle of James, who exhorts his brethren to 'be patient therefore ... unto the coming (*parousia*) of the Lord' (Jas. v. 7). R. V. G. Tasker[1] has some wise words to say on this passage. 'If the Lord's return seems to us to be long delayed, or if we relegate it to such a remote future that it has no effect upon our outlook or way of living, it is clear that it has ceased to be for us a *living* hope; and it may be that we have allowed the doctrine that "He will come again with glory to judge both the quick and the dead" to be whittled away by scepticism, or to be so transmuted into something else, such as the gradual trans- formation of human society by Christian values, that it has ceased to exercise any powerful influence on our lives.'

It is such a 'living hope' in many parts of the world today. For instance, an African pastor in the Congo was welcoming a deputation sent out by the Baptist Missionary Society. He said that they had heard much about the Baptist Missionary Society, and had seen the letters 'B.M.S.' on boxes and

[1] *Commentary on the Epistle of James* (Tyndale Press, 1956), p. 120.

parcels, but had hitherto only a dim idea of 'the Society'. Now it had come to visit them, however, and they gave it their warmest welcome, for this was a great day in their lives. He went on to say that a still greater and more glorious day was coming. They had heard of Christ from His messengers, and read about Him in His book, but one day soon He would come in Person, their eyes would see Him and their hearts would overflow with joy.

TOMORROW?

A missionary in India was speaking to some lepers concerning the Second Advent, and put the question, Do you think He might come tomorrow? The answer came back, 'We don't know, but we hope so'! The thought should not be put aside too lightly. For as the years roll on, the time is drawing nearer, and one day, we know not when, it *will* be 'tomorrow'. When that day comes it will find a world careless and unprepared, 'as in the days that were before the flood' (Mt. xxiv. 38).

In the Olivet discourse the Lord reinforced his fourfold command to watch with the words, 'If the goodman of the house had known in what watch the thief would come, he would have watched' (Mt. xxiv. 43), and He added a blessing on the servant who would be found watching, a blessing which may fall on any one of us who is faithful. This striking simile reverberates through the New Testament; it was part of Paul's teaching in Thessalonica (1 Thes. v. 2), and Peter repeats it (2 Pet. iii. 10). At last in the book of Revelation, as John sees the vision of the seven bowls of wrath which lead up to the consummation, and describes the outpouring of the sixth vial which leads to the drying up of the Euphrates and the going forth of spirits of devils to gather the kings of the earth to the great day of God Almighty, a voice breaks in suddenly, 'Behold, I come as a thief' (Rev. xvi. 15). The speaker can be no other than Jesus, and He adds, 'Blessed is he that watcheth, and keepeth his garments. . . .' The lesson which the Lord Himself drew is sharp and clear, 'Take ye heed, watch and pray: for ye know not when the time is' (Mk. xiii. 33). We ask When? and this is the answer. Or again, 'Be ye therefore ready also: for the Son of man cometh at an hour when ye think not' (Lk. xii. 40). Peter, characteristically, interjects, 'Lord, speakest thou this parable unto us, or even to all?' (Lk. xii. 41). Jesus then makes it general. Blessed is the servant, He says, who at all times is diligent in his Master's service. Watchfulness, prayerfulness, diligence, all these should result from our ignorance of the time. We do not know the time; but we do know our duty.

The classic story of the conversion of Augustine, professor of rhetoric in Rome, illustrates how the near approach of the day of salvation may affect a whole life. It tells how he was musing and lamenting his sins, when he heard the voice of children at play, and one said, '*Tolle, lege*' (take and read). He picked up his Bible and it opened at Romans xiii. 12–14. 'The night is far spent, the day is at hand: let us therefore cast off the works of darkness, and let us put on the armour of light.' These words wrought a change in his life, and the licentious young professor became a humble disciple; and his mother's prayers were answered.[1]

Paul strikes a similar, but yet different, note when writing to the Corinthians, 'brethren, the time is short' (1 Cor. vii. 29). Life is transformed when it is re-interpreted in the light of the brevity of opportunity and the nearness of Christ's coming. 'The nearness and the uncertainty of the time of Christ's coming is the regulative element in the Christian life' (Jonathan Edwards).

'NOT YET'

Though the Lord's discourse left open the time of His coming, it contained hints of delay. There would be deception and persecution, wars and rumours of wars, 'but the end is not yet'. The gospel must be published among all nations, and

[1] *Confessions*, VIII, 12.

this could not be accomplished in a day; Jerusalem would be trodden down by the Gentiles until their time be fulfilled. In the parable of the talents He pictures a master who went 'into a far country' and only returned 'after a long time' (Mt. xxv. 14, 19). Add to this a small, but significant point, that He said, 'then shall they (not 'you') see the Son of man coming'. Before this He had been addressing them in the second person; now He uses the third. (See Luke xxi. 27.)

So far, then, from leading the disciples to expect His immediate return, the Lord prepared them for delay. The preaching of the gospel and the fall of Jerusalem must come first. That Peter well understood; this is proved by his argument in 2 Peter iii. 4ff. The Lord's promise to come is admitted, but there is no slackness on His part. He plans His own timing, whether a thousand years or a day; He will work out His own purpose without hurry and without delay. Part of that purpose will be to bring many more to repentance; there was still scope for the preaching, Repent and believe the gospel. By so doing, the time of His return might be hastened (2 Pet. iii. 12). It is a wonderful letter, and it is, like the other Scriptures, 'written for our learning'.

Jesus said, 'the gospel must first be published among all nations' (Mk. xiii. 10), or, more literally, 'to all the nations must first be heralded the gospel'. This word of divine necessity, and its interpretation by two generations of student missionary volunteers, has been commented upon in chapter II (pp. 24f.). If the question now be put, Has this already been done?, many would give an affirmative, and some a negative answer. The Lord said nothing of conversion; nor is there any promise in the Bible that all will be converted; rather the reverse. There will always be those whose names are written in the Book of Life and those whose names are not. Neither is it stated that every living person must first hear and understand the gospel message. The form of words both in Matthew and Mark cannot be pressed so far as this; they describe a world-wide preaching, and no more. There is still urgent need for the publication of the good news to every creature, by the

printed word to those who can read, and the word of mouth
to all. We may still say with Paul, 'Woe is me, if I preach not
the gospel!'

But this particular sentence we are considering speaks of
'heralding' among all 'nations'. Writing to the Romans, Paul
said, 'But I say, Have they not heard? Yes verily, their sound
'went into all the earth, and their words unto the ends of the
world' (Rom. x. 18). More than a century later, Origen wrote,
The word of the gospel is not yet heard in the East . . . and
what of the Britons and the Germans?'

What would they say of today when printed Scriptures are
distributed in every nation, and in many tribal languages and
dialects? It is difficult to believe that the Lord must needs
delay His return until the process has gone still further.

A note of time may be contained in the words, reported
only by Luke, 'Jerusalem shall be trodden down of the
Gentiles, until the times of the Gentiles be fulfilled' (Lk. xxi.
24). It comes as an appendix to the judgment of the city, and
the treading down apparently refers to the yoke of foreign
rule. The word translated 'times' also means 'opportunity',
and several meanings of the words are possible.[1] They suggest
that the day of opportunity for Israel has ended, and a period
of Gentile oppression, or perhaps of Gentile opportunity has
begun, which will also come to an end. The relationship of
the Jews to Gentile rule, when that is exercised by a Christian
ruler or government, is no simple one. On the whole it would
seem as if the Gentile nations have had their opportunity, and
that there is nothing in this saying to hinder the Lord's return.

Even before the fall of Jerusalem Paul saw a time coming
when 'the fulness of the Gentiles' would be gathered in: but
he makes no mention of Jerusalem. That city could truly be
said to be trodden down by the early Roman emperors, but
after the conversion of Constantine and under the Western
emperors, churches were built and freedom was established.
It then fell into the hands of Arabs and Saracens, but was
delivered from them by the Crusaders, and for a hundred

[1] See above, p. 29.

years governed by Christian kings. Subsequently it came under the Turk, and when Allenby delivered it in 1917 many greeted this as the end of the times of the Gentiles.[1] At the time of writing old Jerusalem is under the rule of Jordan. However interpreted, this saying remains an uncertain criterion as to date.

THE SIGN

Even though the time of our Lord's return be hid from us, we may, along with the disciples, still ask, 'What shall be the sign of these things?' In reply, He told them of certain things that must be, but the end is 'not yet'. Then He gave them a clear sign of the time when their personal safety would be endangered, namely when they saw the temple about to be desecrated (Mk. xiii. 14); then let them flee for safety. Those would be days of affliction such as the world had never seen, words perhaps based on Daniel xii. 1. The context requires these words to be applied to the siege of Jerusalem, days of horror which Josephus described in similar terms. With regard to His own coming, the Lord said, 'But in those days, after that tribulation, the sun shall be darkened, and the moon shall not give her light, And the stars of heaven shall fall, and the powers that are in heaven shall be shaken' (Mk. xiii. 24; cf. Lk. xxi. 25). Is this the sign for which they were asking? The language is that of Old Testament prophecy. It was used by Isaiah (xiii. 10) in respect of judgment about to fall on Babylon, and by Ezekiel in pronouncing a doom on Egypt (Ezk. xxxii. 7, 8); in neither case was it literal, but symbolical of a time of darkness and terror. It was also used by Joel, who predicted an outpouring of the spirit of God (Joel ii. 28–32). This latter passage was cited by Peter as being fulfilled at Pentecost (Acts ii. 16–21). He appears to take the words in Joel as symbolical of a happening that is wonderful and unprecedented.

In Luke's Gospel the words of the Lord run, 'There shall

[1] See above, pp. 29f.

be signs in sun and moon and stars; and upon the earth
distress of nations, in perplexity for the roaring of the sea and
the billows; men fainting for fear, and for expectation of the
things which are coming on the world . . .' (Lk. xxi. 25f., RV).
If perplexity and fear over coming events are the sign, are
they not with us today? They affect even the secular press. A
journalist wrote recently that things have got out of control,
'and that being so, we can only look for some great act of God'.

Taken in their application to great and terrifying human
events, we may indeed have here a 'sign', for the Lord con-
tinues, 'And when these things begin to come to pass, then
look up, and lift up your heads; for your redemption draweth
nigh' (Lk. xxi. 28). It may well be that the Advent will be
preceded by political convulsions and followed by convulsions
in nature itself. We must await the event. In the Epistles we
find Paul warning Timothy that the latter days will be charac-
terized by apostasy and false doctrine (1 Tim. iv. 1–3), and
John saw a sign of the last time in the appearance of 'many
antichrists' (1 Jn. ii. 18).

The diabolical pressure exercised by communist China to
suppress Christianity, and the increase of false doctrine within
the churches may well be signs that we are in the last days. It
is easy perhaps to be too dogmatic in the interpretation of
current events; but it is easier still to lack in vigilance. We
may still hear the Lord saying, 'What I say unto you, I say
unto *all*, Watch.'

CHAPTER IV

HOW AND WHY?

THE MANNER OF HIS RETURN

AS we try to think realistically of the Lord's return, we naturally begin to wonder how it will take place. He Himself said it would be visible, both when talking with the disciples, and in answer to the high priest.[1] He will come openly; there will be no need to seek for Him in the secret chamber, not to go out to the solitude of the wilderness, for 'as the lightning cometh out of the east, and shineth even unto the west; so shall also the coming of the Son of man be' (Mt. xxiv. 27). Words could not be plainer, and they come with a simple grandeur that attests their genuineness.

The visible character of His coming is also inherent in the two words chiefly used to describe it, *parousia*[2] and *epiphaneia*.[3] These words would not be appropriate to describe an inward and spiritual experience. He 'appeared' at His first coming to earth (2 Tim. i. 10), and He will 'appear' again (2 Tim. iv. 8); the second appearing will be as visible as the first. This thought lies behind what Peter writes in his first Epistle. He is addressing those who, like ourselves, had learned to love the Lord, though they had not seen Him (1 Pet. i. 8); they will receive peace and honour when He is revealed (1 Pet. i. 7). His coming will not only be visible but personal. He used, regarding it, that description of Himself which, while indicating His messiahship (see Dn. vii. 13), emphasized His humanity, the 'Son of man'. The two parables, of the Ten Virgins and the Talents, which illustrate His coming, each lead up to the coming of a person, the Bridegroom and the Master, after a period of absence.

When He ascended, the two angelic messengers said, 'this

---

[1] See above, p. 11.   [2] See p. 16.   [3] See pp. 16f.

same Jesus . . . shall so come in like manner as ye have seen him go into heaven' (Acts i. 11). They called them 'men of Galilee', bringing to mind the place where they had companied with Him; He will be the same Person whom they have known on earth. After His resurrection He had taken pains to assure them of His personal identity, by eating with them, showing them His hands and feet, and assuring them that He was no disembodied spirit (Lk. xxiv. 26). It is thus in reality that He will come again. But how far can we carry the literal interpretation of the words 'in like manner'? Some say that He will return to the Mount of Olives, and see a prediction of this in Zechariah xiv. 4. But the scene pictured there of Jehovah summoning all the nations to battle (Zc. xiv. 2) is surely something very different. But if His coming be as the lightning, does it matter 'where'?

Jesus spoke of coming 'with great power and glory'; this alone would create a difference between the manner of His return and the simplicity of His ascension. Can we then take literally Paul's vivid description in 1 Thessalonians iv? Will the clouds be real, or only symbolical of heavenly glory? Shall we hear the 'voice of the archangel' and the 'trump of God'? We should not too easily dismiss these words as purely figurative. The trumpet sounded when the law was given on Sinai (Ex. xix. 13), and it was an angel who announced the Saviour's birth.

It is easier to ask the questions than to give the answers. But we should not give way to doubt, nor let the difficulties deter us from studying the Scriptures. We can agree with one who said, 'I do not know *how* it will be, but I believe I shall meet Him in the air.' Paul said, 'we shall be changed'; and it may be that our present limitations may go, and our faculties be greatly enlarged. We may recall the parable of the caterpillar and the butterfly. As the butterfly described the glory and wonder of the world of space, the poor crawling creature of a two-dimensional experience found it difficult to believe what he was told, or even to conceive it. But it was true; and in due time he became a chrysalis and a butterfly himself and then he proved that it was all such as he had been told. 'O ye of little faith, wherefore do ye doubt?'

'Now are we the sons of God, and it doth not yet appear what we shall be: but we know that, when he shall appear, we shall be like him; for we shall see him as he is' (1 Jn. iii. 2). This is 'the hope' that exists in our hearts. A lady, as she walked past a crippled boy being wheeled in a chair, remarked, 'Poor lad, how sad.' She was surprised when a voice came from the chair, 'It's all right; I shall have *wings* one day, lady!'

So let us look up also, and lift up our heads. It is natural for man to think of heaven as 'above'; and 'our conversation is in heaven; from whence also we look for the Saviour, the Lord Jesus Christ: who shall change our vile body, that it may be fashioned like unto his glorious body' (Phil. iii. 20, 21). Will our eyes be opened to see the angels who do His bidding? It may be, we do not know. So, even though it be beyond our present powers of apprehension, let us continue to sing,

> Lo! He comes, with clouds descending,
> Once for favoured sinners slain;
> Thousand thousand saints attending
> Swell the triumph of His train.

We look to see Him descend 'from heaven' (1 Thes. i. 10). Daniel[1] in his vision saw the 'Son of man' come to the throne of God to be invested with dominion and glory; this was fulfilled in His resurrection and ascension. He is even now 'sitting on the right hand of power' (Mk. xiv. 62), and it is thence that we shall see Him coming.

SCIENCE AND SCRIPTURE

It must be frankly admitted that what we say and sing in church, and believe in our hearts, seems strangely out of keeping with the modern outlook on the stellar universe. We are taught that we are living upon a tiny planet whirling

---

[1] For a thorough treatment of Daniel vii. 13 as a Messianic prophecy, see E. J. Young, *Daniel's Vision of the Son of Man* (Tyndale Press, 1958).

through space at a terrific speed round the sun, beyond which are stars and constellations, visible and invisible. We read of experiments with space travel, rockets shooting up, into and through the 'stratosphere' and reporting conditions there by means of cleverly contrived instruments. Or, in the region of the infinitely small, we read about nuclear fission, protons and electrons, far too small to be seen, but we are assured they are there. And we believe it all. The ordinary person does not understand it, but he accepts it *on faith*. The scientists who know say it is so, and they are credible, honest witnesses, who would not deceive.

Thus we believe, though we cannot understand, the wonders of science. Some of the things seem too strange to be true; but we believe them on the testimony of those we trust, and we go through life accepting much that we cannot explain. We jump on to a trolley-bus without understanding its mechanism; and how many viewers have the slightest idea of how the picture on the television screen comes to be there? When we come to apply these thoughts to our present prob-lem, let us reflect a little upon what constitutes modern science, and recognize, first, that it is not the *advance* of science which constitutes our difficulty; if anything it is the reverse. Fifty years ago the idea of many people seeing, simultaneously, an event many miles distant would have been declared scientifically impossible. As a leading scientist has said, 'the physical impossibility of one era is the commonplace of the next'. The advance of science sometimes makes faith easier.

When we come to think of it, the difficulty of thinking of heaven as above us, and beyond the clouds, was just as real to Isaac Newton as to ourselves. He knew about the planets, and formulated the laws of their motion. Yet he was a firm believer in holy Scripture and even a writer on prophecy. He has been followed by a long line of scientific investigators, Faraday, Clerk-Maxwell, Lord Kelvin and many others, who also at the same time were earnest Christians. Yet nearly all the difficulties which are raised today were well-known to them. If they believed the Bible, may we not do the same?

They would tell us that science has its limits, and within these limits, is to be believed. But the Scriptures also can be believed; there is no contradiction between the two.

A former generation had as a textbook in advanced physics a book entitled *Natural Philosophy* by Thomson and Tait. The former, afterwards Lord Kelvin, on many public occasions made profession of his Christian faith. His colleague, Professor Tait, published an interesting book, *The Unseen Universe*. Starting from the standpoint of pure science he maintained that in more than one direction science led up to a boundary which it could not pass, but which necessitated belief in an unknown region which lay beyond. He deduced that science itself points to the existence of an unseen universe, such as that which the Bible calls heaven. We therefore also may believe that it was into heaven that Jesus Christ passed at His ascension. The reader who believes this on the authority of the Word of God will find himself in good company.

From a different and entirely modern point of view, Sir Arthur Eddington, himself a Christian and a member of the Society of Friends, argued in his book, *The Nature of the Physical World*, for the existence of a spiritual world just as 'real', though different from, the physical. But the two have their 'boundaries', and while the Christian has the right to believe in heaven, he is warned against trying to reconcile it with Einstein's relativity theory.[1] 'Science', he has said elsewhere, 'uncompromisingly rejects the proposition that that which no one observes does not exist.' We may rest content with the assurance that the heaven to which Christ ascended and whence He will return is beyond our vision but not beyond our belief.

We read that the Advent will be 'with power', which suggests the supernatural. In this we may take encouragement from an unlikely source. It was Professor Huxley, the nineteenth-century protagonist of Agnosticism, who wrote concerning the miraculous, 'We are not justified in the

[1] See pp. 333–347. In a later book, *New Pathways of Science* (1935), he defends these views from attack by Bertrand Russell (see pp. 306, 317).

a priori assertion that the order of nature, as experience has revealed it to us, cannot change.'[1]

We are indeed justified both in believing the miracles of the Gospels, and in allowing for a like display of supernatural power at the Lord's return. It is as easy to believe that He will be accompanied by angels then, as that the angels appeared to the shepherds at His birth. He may speak to us then, and as it was on the day of Pentecost, we may each hear the message in our own tongue. The power of God, which raised Jesus from the dead, will suffice also to raise those who are 'asleep in Jesus' at His coming. As God gave to Him a resurrection body which possessed new power, so He will give to us who are alive and remain, new and glorious bodies like unto His.

Let us therefore not be deterred by difficulties, but look forward with expectant hope as we would to a visit to a foreign land, whose beauties we can only dimly comprehend until they burst upon our view.

REALIZED ESCHATOLOGY

What will *follow* upon the *parousia* will be considered later. We will close this chapter by thinking of the reasons given for this glad event.

A new type of teaching, which evades all difficulties by denying the personal Advent altogether, goes by the name of Realized Eschatology.[2] In simple English this means that the only 'coming' of Jesus Christ is that which is already realized in Christian experience; 'all that the Church hoped for in the second coming of Christ is already given in its present experience of Christ through the Spirit'.[3]

That Paul believed in an actual return of Christ is not denied, but it is said that he revised this opinion as he grew

---

[1] *Science and Christian Tradition*, p. 204.

[2] See C. H. Dodd, *Parables of the Kingdom* (Nisbet, 1935); *New Testament Studies* (Manchester, 1954).

[3] C. H. Dodd, *The Apostolic Teaching and its Developments* (London, 1936), p. 174. See articles by Professor G. E. Ladd in the *Evangelical Quarterly* of April and July 1958, where this view is stated and criticized.

older and wiser.[1] The integrity of the second Epistle to the
Corinthians is also challenged. Scepticism is carried still further
in a volume by J. A. T. Robinson,[2] in which the Gospel
records are discredited because of what they contain of em-
bellishment and addition. The words of Jesus in Mark xiii.
24–27 are unacceptable because they are 'untypical of how
Jesus uses Scripture'.[3] It is admitted that 'the Church expected
Jesus. That is not open to dispute'.[4] But it is maintained that
this was not part of the original apostolic tradition; it crept in
at an early stage through misinterpretation of Old Testament
prophecy and certain sayings of Jesus Christ. He never really
promised to come again. His appearance in Galilee was a
'vision', and the truth of the ascension as recorded in Acts i.
1–11 is denied: the story is due to Luke's endeavour to
'harmonize' diverse 'traditions'.[5]

What the early Christians mistakenly looked for in the
parousia is to be found in 'the liturgical life of the Church'[6] and
the real presence of Christ in the Sacrament. The ordinary
reader lays the book aside with impatience, mixed with some
wonderment as to how the author can continue to recite the
Apostles' Creed.

Of a different character is the 'existential' philosophy of
Rudolf Bultmann. He regards all miracles, including the
resurrection and the ascension of our Lord, as 'myths' which
must be cleared away before the gospel can be rendered
acceptable to the modern man. Readers who are interested

[1] See above, pp. 32f.

[2] *Jesus and His Coming* (SCM, 1957). Somewhat similar views are
expressed, but with a strong admixture of mysticism, in a book by
J. E. Fison, *The Christian Hope* (SCM, 1954).

[3] *Op. cit.*, p. 56. On the other side, see N. B. Stonehouse, *The Witness
of Matthew and Mark to Christ* (Tyndale Press, 1959), pp. 113f., 233–242.

[4] *Op. cit.*, p. 16.

[5] *Op. cit.*, pp. 132, 177.

[6] *Op. cit.*, p. 185. Doubtless the liturgy of the Prayer Book is a great
asset; but those who have listened to the liturgy of the Roman or
Greek Orthodox Churches chanted in a foreign tongue to a group of
peasants or refugees, will fail to identify it with the Second Advent.

will find this new theory expounded and confuted in a pamphlet by P. E. Hughes.[1]

These views, which 'spiritualize' the return of Christ, to make it mean something quite different to the plain meaning of Christ's own words, may be traced in part to a reaction against the views of Albert Schweitzer,[2] who insisted on their real meaning, but described Christ as a purely human figure, who believed that He would return again soon, but was mistaken. It is a relief to turn again from such sophisticated speculation to the simple record of the New Testament writers. Luke's reputation as a careful and accurate historian will not be so easily shaken,[3] and his account of the ascension must be accepted as true.

THE PURPOSE OF HIS RETURN

A group of young Bible students held a discussion upon the purposes of the Lord's return, and listed them as follows: (1) To gather living and dead Christians together. (2) To make us perfect. (3) To inaugurate the Millennium (some doubt expressed as to when). (4) To destroy all evil and the devil. (5) To destroy the earth and bring judgment. (6) To inaugurate the new heaven and the new earth. (7) That God at last may be supreme. It is an interesting list, for every element in it can be justified by Scripture. Among these aims the first is that most immediately connected with the *parousia*.

In the parable of the wheat and the tares, in the Lord's prophetic discourse, and in the upper room, Jesus announced as a primary object of His return the gathering of His redeemed children to Himself, that they might be with Him. This is the first and primary object of His coming; and if He cares for our company, how much more should our hearts leap at the thought of being with Him! Thus He had wished to 'gather' (the same word is used) the people of Jerusalem,

[1] *Scripture and Myth* (Tyndale Press, 1956).

[2] *The Quest for the Historical Jesus* (1910; English Translation, Black, 1945).

[3] See Sir William Ramsay, *Luke the Historian.*

but they would not (Lk. xiii. 34). Paul had learned that this was the Lord's purpose, for he beseeches the Thessalonians by the coming (*parousia*) of our Lord Jesus Christ, and by our gathering together (*episunagōgē*) unto Him (2 Thes. ii. 1).

He has gone to prepare a place for us, and will come again and receive us unto Himself, that where He is there we may be also (Jn. xiv. 3). What wonderful love! Our hearts have no need to be troubled. Then shall we also 'appear with him in glory' (Col. iii. 4). What a gathering that will be! He sent forth the apostles to witness to the 'uttermost part of the earth' (Acts i. 8), and He will send His angels to gather the converts 'from the uttermost part of the earth to the uttermost part of heaven' (Mk. xiii. 27); none will be missed out. At the advent of an earthly monarch some of us have been spectators; but at the Advent of Jesus we shall all be partakers, even the humblest of us.

This gathering together will also be a gathering out of God's own chosen ones (Mk. xiii. 27); 'the one shall be taken, and the other left' (Lk. xvii. 30–36). As it was revealed to Paul, 'the dead in Christ shall rise first: then we which are alive and remain shall be caught up together with them in the clouds, to meet the Lord in the air: and so shall we ever be with the Lord' (1 Thes. iv. 16, 17). This has been called 'the rapture of the Church', and by some, 'the secret rapture', though the Scripture does not call it secret or so describe it.

At first the thought of this separation seems to strike a discordant note. It is disturbing to think of ourselves meeting with the Lord, while others, perhaps our friends, even members of our family, are left behind. Nevertheless there is no escape from the division, everywhere to be found in the New Testament, between those who accept and those who reject the offer of salvation. The thought should spur us to action in our effort to win others; we must be 'instant in season, out of season' to preach the word (2 Tim. iv. 2). As to those who are left, we are told nothing; but God is both merciful and just, and we may safely leave the fate of others in His hands.

Paul then tells us, 'by the word of the Lord', that we shall be 'caught up together with them in the clouds, to meet the Lord in the air' (I Thes. iv. 15, 17). Does this strike us as strange and bizarre? At least it signifies a region which is above, and better than, this present earth. Jesus had spoken of the place where we would be with Him as His Father's house, in which were many resting-places. It is well that we should follow these examples and picture the scene as graphically as we can; but the essential fact is that we shall ever be with the Lord, and this fills our hearts with joyful expectation.

But are we fit to dwell with Him? Here below we strive after holiness, but when we have done our best we know that we are 'unprofitable servants'. We are taught that our salvation from sin, which is begun now, will be perfected then. The Epistle to the Hebrews teaches a vital connection between the atoning work of Christ upon the cross, and its completion when He will come again the second time 'without sin unto salvation' (Heb. ix. 26, 28). The work of grace in our hearts is the work of Christ from beginning to end. He is well able to complete it, 'to present you faultless before the presence of his glory' (Jude 24). Blameless and faultless might seem to be enough; but John goes further when he says that 'when he shall appear, we shall be like him; for we shall see him as he is' (I Jn. iii. 2). He will even give us then a new body, spiritual, incorruptible and immortal (I Cor. xv. 53). That will be victory! This is a prospect to fill every believer with exultant joy. But there is yet more even than this, for He brings rewards with Him.

'Behold, I come quickly; and my reward is with me, to give every man according as his work shall be' (Rev. xxii. 12). Paul knows of 'a crown of righteousness, which the Lord . . . shall give . . . unto all them that love his appearing' (2 Tim. iv. 8), and to those who feed His sheep He will give 'a crown of glory' (I Pet. v. 4). Surely 'eye hath not seen, nor ear heard, neither have entered into the heart of man, the things which God hath prepared for them that love him' (I Cor. ii. 9).

Other things connected with the Lord's return are dealt

with in the book of Revelation, in some ways the most interesting of all the books in the Bible. There will be the destruction of the Lord's enemies (Rev. xix. 20), the binding of Satan for a thousand years (xx. 2), a period following (xx. 7); and after the burning of every evil thing, the creation of new heavens and a new earth, and the establishment of the new Jerusalem. The Revelation of St. John is a soul-stirring book, which exercises a strange charm over the life of one who studies it in a humble spirit. Our next chapter will be devoted to a brief introduction to it and its teaching on the Lord's return.

CHAPTER V

THE BOOK OF REVELATION

THE Apocalypse (lit. 'unveiling'), or the book of Revelation, is at once one of the most fascinating, the most difficult and yet most spiritually rewarding of all the books in the Bible. It forms a sort of epilogue to all which precedes it. The Old Testament tells the story of man's creation and fall, and leads up to the promise of a Saviour. The Gospels contain the life and teaching of Jesus when on earth, and conclude with His death and resurrection. After this the Acts and Epistles describe the spread of the gospel and contain the apostolic teaching. Finally, this book is as a message from the throne, where Jesus sits at the right hand of God the Father. And it begins and ends with the message that He is coming again. It is not such a difficult book as may at first appear, if the reader will adhere to the main lines of its teaching, and not stray into by-paths of ingenious speculations and curious calculations. 'There are some', said Bengel, 'who wretchedly mishandle this book with restless curiosity.'

Our immediate object in this chapter is to recommend its study and endeavour to help in its understanding. We begin with a consideration of its origin and purpose.

ORIGIN AND PURPOSE

Early tradition is unanimous (Justin Martyr, Papias, Irenaeus) in assigning its authorship to John the Apostle, although in the third century doubts arose, mainly for doctrinal reasons.[1] The style indeed contrasts strangely with that of the Gospel

---

[1] The evidence, for and against, is given *in extenso* in Alford's commentary, pp. 198–228. Professor Swete leaves the question open, but says that the evidence of the synoptic Gospels and the 'main current of Christian tradition' favour the apostolic authorship.

and Epistles, but this can be accounted for by the difference of time, circumstance and subject. It was written at a time of intense persecution, probably in the reign of Domitian, when John had been exiled to Patmos for his faith (i. 9), for which others had suffered martyrdom (ii. 10, 13), and this is reflected in the language, the imagery and the spirit of the book. It is no wonder that John longed to see Jesus coming (i. 7). Afterwards he was released, and lived a few years in peace at Ephesus, where his Gospel was written at the urgent request of his followers.

The book takes the form of an Epistle addressed to seven churches in Asia Minor, to whom his name and person were evidently familiar and his authority unquestioned. Sir William Ramsay has shown[1] how closely the letters in chapters ii and iii reflect the conditions then obtaining in each of the centres named. Emperor worship was no unimportant feature in the life of Asia Minor; and it is thought that the 'mark' of Revelation xiii. 16 refers to some sort of certificate granted to those who conformed, which enabled them to buy and sell in the public market. The temptation to give way was therefore severe. Jesus had said to the twelve in the upper room, 'In the world ye shall have tribulation: but be of good cheer; I have overcome the world' (Jn. xvi. 33); and now tribulation has befallen them, and 'overcome' is one of the watchwords of this book. John had also heard Him say, 'ye shall be witnesses' (Acts i. 8), and the words 'record', 'witness', 'testify', 'testimony', 'martyr' (all the same word in Greek) constantly recur, forming a fruitful field of study.

There are other connections with the life of St. John. At the beginning of his discipleship he had heard the Baptist say, 'Behold the Lamb of God . . .', and the words were treasured in his memory. He was present at the Passover service and witnessed the crucifixion. Now in Patmos he sees in vision 'a Lamb as it had been slain' (v. 6), and henceforth 'the Lamb' dominates his thought. He listened to Jesus' prophetic words on the Mount of Olives, and the Apocalypse has been de-

[1] *The Letters to the Seven Churches of Asia* (Hodder and Stoughton).

scribed as a 'commentary' on that discourse. Again He stood on the mount as a cloud received Him out of their sight; and now 'in like manner' he beholds Him come (i. 7). 'See! He is coming!—with clouds!'

The purpose of the book is plainly stated in the opening verses, namely, to 'shew unto his servants things which must shortly come to pass' (i. 1), and these include the Lord's return. Thus Jesus had prepared the seventy for what would befall them, and had likewise instructed the twelve disciples before His death. Now, in this book, He teaches all those who love His appearing how to take heed, to watch and to pray.

STRUCTURE AND CONTENT

A simple outline of the book, showing its general structure, can be set down as follows:

i. Prologue. 'Behold He cometh' (i. 1–8).
ii. Vision of Christ. Individual messages of rebuke and encouragement to the seven churches (i. 9–iii).
iii. Vision of God on the throne, and acclamation of Christ the Victor (iv and v).
iv. Visions of judgment and salvation, seven seals, seven trumpets and seven vials. Continuous warfare till Christ rides to victory (vi–xix).
v. Satan bound for 1,000 years, and cast into the fire. Judgment of mankind (xx).
vi. The new Jerusalem (xxi–xxii. 6).
vii. Epilogue. 'Behold, I come quickly' (xxii. 7–21).

Let us now consider this in detail. After the prologue, John describes a vision of Christ, all glorious, standing in the midst of the churches, alive for evermore. He is bidden to write special messages to each of the seven churches. These follow in chapters ii and iii, each concluding with a familiar saying of Jesus (see Mk. iv. 9; Lk. xiv. 35). Next (iv. 1) a door is opened in heaven and a voice bids John to 'come up hither', whither the reader follows him, and sees God on His throne surrounded by twenty-four elders seated, and four beasts before the throne engaged in worship and praise.

We next see a roll, covered with writing front and back, but sealed with seven seals, which no-one is found worthy to open. But one of the elders cries, 'behold, the Lion of the tribe of Juda, the Root of David, hath prevailed to open the book' (v. 5). But when John looks, he only sees a little lamb as it had been slain; but that Lamb is in the midst of the throne, the seat of all majesty and power. The mystic roll in chapter v is opened, but never read, nor are its contents disclosed. It has been interpreted as (i) the all-wise decrees and judgments of God (Andrews), (ii) future world-history, (iii) God's documentary covenant with Jesus Christ, to accept His atonement for sin. But since we are not told, it is not necessary for us to know.

The opening of the first six seals is followed by a parenthesis (chapter vii). John witnesses the sealing of the servants of God, 12,000 from each of the tribes of Israel, and then a vision of a great multitude of the redeemed of all nations. The sealing denotes God's ownership and care; His servants will be preserved through every earthly trial, and will be no less under His shepherd care hereafter.

Much has been written about the 'great tribulation' (*tēs thlipseōs tēs megalēs*) of Revelation vii. 14. By the majority of 'futurist' interpreters it is aligned with similar expressions in Daniel xii. 1 and Jeremiah xiii. 19, 24, and interpreted as a period of time during which the events prophesied in Revelation viii–xix would occur.[1] But is it possible that this can have been its original meaning? The word occurs more than forty times in the New Testament. Tribulation is the lot of all Christians (Acts xiv. 22), and they can rejoice in it (Rom. v. 3). The context of Revelation vii. 14 applies the words to Christians of all races and all ages.[2]

Upon the opening of the seventh seal, there is an interval of

[1] See note in the Scofield Bible, and G. E. Ladd, *The Blessed Hope*, p. 71.
[2] See Swete, *in loc.*

solemn silence, after which the first six trumpets are blown, each portending a 'woe' (chapters viii and ix). John is now (chapter x) commanded to eat a little book and to prophesy, as were Jeremiah (Je. xv. 16) and Ezekiel (Ezk. iii. 1). He has a vision of Jerusalem (chapter xi) where two witnesses prophesy for forty-two months and are then slain by a beast from the abyss. But after three and a half days they rise up again and ascend to heaven in a cloud.

Further visions follow in chapters xii and xiii. A woman clothed with the sun is persecuted by a red dragon, her child is caught up to the throne of God, and she herself receives protection. Two beasts are seen to arise, one out of the sea to whom the dragon gives authority; and another from the earth, who is also called the false prophet (chapter xiii). Next a Lamb is seen, standing on Mount Zion, with 144,000 followers. As this vision fades, John sees one 'like the Son of man', on a cloud, with a sharp sickle, and He reaps the harvest of the earth. Then an angel is seen, also with a sickle, who reaps the grapes and fills up 'the winepress of the wrath of God' (chapter xiv). Chapter xv introduces seven angels having seven vials of the wrath of God, which in chapter xvi they pour out upon the earth. During the sixth a voice breaks in saying, 'Behold, I come as a thief' (xvi. 15). The outpouring of the seventh vial is accompanied by a voice saying, 'It is done', on which follow lightnings, earthquakes and a great hail. In chapters xvii and xviii Rome comes into view under the figure of a scarlet woman, whose name is Babylon the great (xvii. 1, 5, 9). Her kings make war on the Lamb, who overcomes them. Babylon falls and the saints rejoice.

The scene moves to heaven in chapter xix where a multitude praise God and announce the marriage of the Lamb. The Word of God appears in human form, seated on a white horse with His armies, against whom the kings of the earth make war. He overcomes them, and the Beast and the false prophet are cast into a lake of fire.

Chapter xx tells of a thousand years, or 'Millennium', during which Satan is bound, and 'the souls of them that were beheaded for the witness of Jesus' (xx. 4) live and reign with Christ. At the close Satan is loosed for a season, to deceive the nations and gather them to battle. Fire from heaven destroys them, and Satan himself is cast into the lake of fire. John now sees 'a great white throne, and him that sat on it, from whose face the earth and the heaven fled away' (xx. 11). All the dead are raised, the books are opened, and they are judged according to their works. This is the end of sin and evil. The two closing chapters picture new heavens and a new earth in which the Lamb is the light, and wherein is the river of life and the tree of life. The epilogue has as its centre the promise, 'Behold, I come quickly'.

The themes of the Millennium, the great enemy and the judgment will be developed in the following chapters. When we consider the book as a whole we see how fit an ending it forms to the biblical record. Genesis opens with the creation of the heavens and the earth, man in the garden of Eden, the serpent, the fall of man and paradise lost. Revelation builds upon the atoning death and resurrection of Christ, describes how He bruises the serpent's head and completes the redemption of mankind; God creates new heavens and a new earth and paradise is regained. The background alternates between earth and heaven; and we see angels ascending and descending, as Jacob did at Bethel. We learn that heaven is nearer to earth than we thought. Above all, 'we see Jesus . . . crowned with glory and honour' (Heb. ii. 9), first among His believing people, then on the throne, then reaping the harvest, then as the Word of God riding to victory, and finally as the heavenly Bridegroom about to be united with His bride, the Church, the city of God.

It is a most exhilarating book!

SYMBOLISM

The Apocalypse is delightfully full of symbolism and imagery, the appreciation of which adds to the pleasure and profit which are derived from its study. The meaning of many of the symbols lies on the surface, the glory of gold, the purity of white robes, the fierce power of wild beasts, the wreaths for victory and the diadem for royalty. Some are explained in the context, the seven candlesticks are seven churches (i. 20); the red dragon is none other than that old serpent, the devil (xii. 9). Many have their origin in the Old Testament[1] and the clue to their significance can be found by using a concordance or reference Bible; thus, for the 'lion of the tribe of Judah', see Genesis xlix. 9; for the Lamb, go back to Exodus xii. 3.

A symbolical value often attaches to the numbers; four stands for humanity or the created world, seven for perfection, twelve for covenant relationship, a thousand for a multitude.[2] So the seven eyes of Revelation v. 6 denote divine insight. On the other hand, the number seven applied to the churches is quite literal. In this case the distinction is easy; but sometimes it is difficult to know where symbol ends and literal meaning begins. It is then possible to be over-literal, in bondage to the letter; or so to 'spiritualize' the meaning that the original sense is lost, and something different substituted.

It is by considering the context, and comparing Scripture with Scripture, that a right decision can be reached. When the question affects belief or conduct, the Holy Spirit will guide. Where it concerns only the interpretation of some future happening we may with patience await the event.

SYSTEMS OF INTERPRETATION

In the first three Christian centuries the symbols used by John were interpreted spiritually. The beast of Revelation xiii was the persecuting Roman power, and Rome was the Babylon of Revelation xvii. The early return of Christ was expected to

[1] In his commentary Swete gives 278 references to the Old Testament. Many of these are from Daniel (see p. clii). An interesting study of the relationship of the two books, from a pre-millennial point of view, is contained in *Daniel and Revelation* by Joseph Tanner (Hodder and Stoughton, 1898).

[2] On the interpretation of the periods of days and years in Daniel and Revelation, see pp. 29f.

be followed by the Millennial reign. Today it is customary to speak of three systems of interpretation, the historicist, the futurist and the preterist. Of these the first regards the book as a prophecy of what would befall the Church from the time of writing to the end of the world. It was held by many of the Reformers, and by such scholars as Isaac Newton, Bengel and Hengstenberg. It was elaborated in the last century in *Horae Apocalypticae* by E. B. Elliott. It can be seen in a compendious form in a book by Dr. B. F. C. Atkinson, entitled *The War with Satan*.[1] In his exposition, for example, chapter vi forecasts the decline of the Roman Empire, chapters x and xi the Reformation period, and the end of chapter xvi brings us up to the time in which we are now living. The persecuting power, with its voice of blasphemy, points to the Church of Rome. Some modern evangelical expositors interpret the visions as prophetic of the Christian era and events still future but in rather more general terms. For them the seven seals, the seven trumpets, and the seven vials are not in sequence, but parallel, and each leads up to the time of the end.[2]

The futurist system takes various forms. It will be found expounded with scholarship and moderation in *Crucial Questions about the Kingdom of God* by G. E. Ladd,[3] and in a rather more popular form by Erich Sauer in his book *From Eternity to Eternity*.[4] It takes a definite shape, known as 'dispensationalism', in the notes to the Scofield Bible (see below, pp. 70f.). According to this latter view the letters to the seven churches are taken to signify seven periods of church history. The call, 'Come up hither' in Revelation iv. 1 is interpreted as the fulfilment of 1 Thessalonians iv. 14–17, the 'rapture' of the Church.[5] The basis of this view is that the visions of Revelation vi to xix are an adumbration of what will happen in the latter days. It will be a period of 'the great tribulation', the three and

---

[1] *Protestant Truth Society*, 1940.
[2] See W. Hendriksen, *More than Conquerors* (Tyndale Press, 1940).
[3] Eerdmans, Grand Rapids, 1952.   [4] Paternoster Press, 1954.
[5] This pre-tribulation view of the rapture is controverted by G. E. Ladd in his book, *The Blessed Hope*.

a half years being a reference to the latter part of the seven foretold in Daniel ix. 27.[1] It will fulfil prophecies such as those found in Jeremiah xxx. 7, Daniel xii. 1 and elsewhere. It is the Jewish people who, having returned to Palestine in unbelief, will undergo these trials at the hands of the antichrist. At the end of the three and a half years, Christ will return to earth '*with* His saints' as pictured in chapter xix. He will then set up the throne of David in Jerusalem and there reign for a thousand years.

The preterist view limits the application of the prophecy to the two or three first centuries, thus reducing the predictive element. A modified statement of this position can be found in Professor Swete's commentary. The author maintains the inspiration of the book, and looks 'for fulfilment of St. John's prophetic words in times yet to come',[2] while connecting the greatest part of the book with the destinies of the Roman Empire.

Some student may ask, How can I tell which system to adopt? In reply we can say that full and convinced adherence to any system can only be the result of patient study. But such adherence is not essential to an understanding of the spiritual teaching; indeed the book of Revelation was studied, and commentaries upon it written, for centuries before these systems were formulated. For the systems are not mutually exclusive. From the preterist system we may learn the importance of discerning its application to the early centuries, from the historicist to be on the look out for its connection with church history, and from the futurist to have added zest in looking for signs of the Saviour's coming.

REVELATION AND THE SECOND ADVENT

Some reference to the Advent is to be expected in a book

[1] In the I.V.F. *New Bible Commentary*, Professor E. J. Young mentions his interpretation of Daniel ix. 27 but rejects it in favour of the traditional view, namely that 'Messiah will cause the Jewish sacrifices to cease by means of His death, and He will do this in the midst of the seventh week.' [2] See p. cxviii.

which repeatedly describes itself as a 'prophecy' (i. 3, xxii. 7, 10, 18; cf. x. 11); a word which includes both preaching and prediction. Its predictive character is made clear in i. 1, 19 and iv. 1. It belongs to the nature of prophecy to be like 'a light that shineth in a dark place, until the day dawn' (2 Pet. i. 19), affording the traveller sufficient light to guide his footsteps on the way, and encouraging him to look for increasing light until the morning star (Rev. xxii. 16) heralds the day.

At the beginning (see i. 7) John calls upon the reader to share his vision. 'Behold, he cometh with clouds', for so he had heard Jesus say (Mk. xiii. 26). He proceeds, 'and every eye shall see him, and they also which pierced him'; again John remembers what he had seen on that fateful day when Jesus was crucified (Jn. xix. 34). 'And all kindreds of the earth shall wail because of him'; some with hostile fears, says Bengel, and some with penitential tears. John adds his affirmation both in Greek, *nai* ('Even so'), and in Hebrew, *amen*.

The passage confirms the general teaching of the New Testament, that the Lord's coming will be a visible event. It is difficult to accept the view, referred to above, that Revelation iv. 1 is a prediction of the Advent. The words 'after this' merely introduce a new section,[1] and do not signify a lapse of time; the vision of a 'door' does not fit this application, and there is no mention either of the Lord or His people. But there are other places in which Jesus Himself announces His return. The first of these is in the letter to Thyatira, 'That which ye have already hold fast till I come' (ii. 25). There is also an assurance in the letter to Philadelphia, the church for which He has no word of blame. 'Behold, I come quickly: hold that fast which thou hast, that no man take thy crown' (iii. 11). What a word is this for persecuted Christians, such as our fellow-believers in communist China today, who are under such pressure to deny their faith.

We hear the voice of Jesus again in the middle of the book. John is describing the pouring out of the seven vials, and as he reaches the sixth, the narrative is interrupted by the words,

[1] See vii. 1, 9, xv. 5, xviii. 1.

'Behold, I come as a thief. Blessed is he that watcheth, and keepeth his garments . . .' (xvi. 15), and the announcement of Armageddon follows (verse 16). It is Jesus, reiterating the warning in the form which had so impressed the disciples.

When we come to the last chapter of Revelation, and of the Bible itself, we meet with a threefold 'Behold, I come quickly'. The first of these is accompanied by a blessing upon him 'that keepeth the sayings of the prophecy of this book' (xxii. 7; cf. i. 3), a blessing still available for him who will claim it. A second time He says, 'Behold, I come quickly; and my reward is with me' (xxii. 12), and finally once more, 'Surely I come quickly' (xxii. 20). Strange, is it not, that we need so much reminding?

Apart from these direct statements there are visions which relate to the Advent. In chapter xiv John describes a vision of a white cloud, on which was seated one like unto the Son of man, with a golden diadem upon His head, and in His hand a sharp sickle (verse 14). An angel from the heavenly temple bids Him thrust in His hand and reap, for the time is come; and thereupon 'the earth was reaped' (verses 15, 16). John had heard the Lord use the simile of a harvest in the parable of the wheat and tares. Here there is no word about tares; but a second vision follows of an angel who gathered the vine of the earth and cast it into 'the winepress of the wrath of God'. As in the parable, the ministry of grace is in the hands of the Son of man, that of wrath is committed to the angels.

In chapter xix we hear voices announcing that 'the marriage of the Lamb is come, and his wife hath made herself ready' (xix. 7). But the imagery swiftly changes; the heaven is opened and one appears riding on a white horse, and crowned with many diadems. The description tallies with that of Jesus in chapter i and we are told that 'his name is called The Word of God' (xix. 13), a wonderful name, repeated in the opening chapter of John's Gospel. His character as 'the Lamb' falls into the background (though His vesture is dipped in blood); He is going forth to war, and is followed by the armies in heaven. Against Him come the beast, the kings of the earth and their armies; but they are overcome and consigned to the lake of fire. So the present age seems to end.

It is hazardous to interpret the order of the visions in the Apocalypse in terms of chronological sequence; but the visions which we have just noted have been considered by commentators both ancient and modern to relate to the Advent. Chapter xxi opens with the creation of new heavens and a new earth; and it is natural to place the visions of chapter xx in between. After the Millennium (which will be considered in the following chapter), the great judgment of all mankind, and the final end of death and Hades, John sees a new heaven and a new earth, and the holy city, the new Jerusalem, descend out of heaven as a bride adorned for her husband (xxi. 1, 2). The metaphors are strangely combined but their meaning is plain; the city is both the people of God, and their dwelling-place; the symbolic number twelve predominates. All evil is now left behind; the city is reserved for those whose names are written in the Lamb's book of life, and the Lamb is its light.

In chapter xxii the symbolism changes, though the Lamb is still on the throne. We are back in the garden of Eden; but there is no sin, and there is free access to the tree of life (cf. Gn. iii. 24). Here 'his servants shall serve him: and they shall see his face' (xxii. 3, 4); and those who love Him ask no more than this. Jesus speaks again, and with His threefold promise to come quickly, the revelation comes to an end.

The Apocalypse is in a double sense 'the revelation of Jesus Christ' for it not only contains a message *from* Him, but a most revealing picture *of* Him. He is revealed to us as the Son of man in the midst of the churches, as the first and the last, as the Son of God, as the holy and true that hath the key of David, and as the beginning of the creation of God. He is the Lion of Judah, the Lamb that was slain, the Word of God, the root and offspring of David, the bright and morning star; or simply Jesus, so named at His birth into the world.[1]

[1] Rev. i. 13, ii. 8, 18, iii. 7, 14, v. 5, 6, xix. 13, 16, xxii. 16, etc

Let anyone who has learned to know Jesus in the Gospels and in Christian experience, study each of these titles in its context, and he will find himself uplifted to the heavenly places, where Jesus is now seated at God's right hand.

When Dr. J. Church was asked what was the secret of the Revival in Ruanda, that movement which has so powerfully affected the lives of thousands of African Christians, he gave the answer, 'It is simply Jesus.' The same answer might be given to the question, What is the object of the book of Revelation? Search out what it has to say about Jesus, and you will have the key to its meaning.

CHAPTER VI

THE MILLENNIUM

MANY people have been turned aside from the study of the Millennium because of the amount of controversy and curious speculation to which it has given rise. But this very fact is a witness to the importance which Bible students have attached to it, and to the problems which it raises. Among these is its proper relation to the Second Advent, whether it pictures what will lead up to that event, or what will follow after it; what is meant by the binding of Satan, and the reign of the saints, and how these are related to the teaching of Christ and the New Testament generally.

In this chapter our aim will be to understand the original meaning of Revelation xx. 1-7, and then to learn from it lessons for life today. A further question, which the events of the past forty years have brought into prominence, is what part, if any, the land of Palestine and the Jewish people will play, before or after the Lord's return. We may not be able to answer all the questions that arise, but it is our duty to learn what the Scripture teaches us about them, for all Scripture is written for our learning.

The book of Revelation is a prophecy (i. 3, xxii. 7), and as is the case with all prophecy, we shall best understand its application to our own time if we begin by enquiring what it meant to the writer and to those for whom it was originally intended.

Let us therefore look at what is said in Revelation xx concerning the 'thousand years'. The phrase occurs six times in Revelation xx. 1-7. We may group them as follows:

a. An angel laid hold of the dragon, the devil, and bound him for a thousand years (2), in order that 'he should deceive the nations no more, till the thousand years should be fulfilled: and after that he must be loosed a little season' (3). 'And when the thousand years are expired, Satan shall be loosed out of his prison (7), and shall go out to deceive the nations. . . .'

b. 'I saw the souls of them that were beheaded for the witness of Jesus, and for the word of God, and which had not worshipped the beast, neither his image, neither had received his mark upon their foreheads, or in their hands; and they lived and reigned with Christ a thousand years' (4). 'Blessed and holy is he that hath part in the first resurrection: . . . they shall be priests of God and of Christ, and shall reign with him a thousand years' (6).

c. 'But the rest of the dead lived not again until the thousand years were finished' (5).

There can be no doubt that to John in Patmos the vision proclaimed a complete reversal of the then desperate situation. Satan had the world powers under his leadership: that would cease. The martyrs who had been executed would rise again, with other confessors. Whereas now the Roman power judged the Christians, then the power of judgment would be given to Christ and His followers. Instead of the Roman imperium, Christ would reign with His saints. *Everything* would be changed in their favour, and this, not for a brief period but for long years.

This meaning, or something very like it, would be what the little company in Pergamos or Thyatira would understand as that which God was revealing to them by His servant John. But we are not left to conjecture upon this question, for we have available the testimony of various second-century writers that this was the general interpretation given to it in their day.

Eusebius records that Papias, who had known some of the apostles, had taught that after the resurrection the kingdom of Christ would be established bodily on earth for a thousand years. Justin Martyr, in his dialogue with Trypho, wrote that Christians knew that there would be a bodily resurrection and that they would dwell in Jerusalem a thousand years and rule and increase as was foretold by Ezekiel and in Isaiah lxv. 17–21. He adds, 'a certain man among us, John by name, one of the apostles of Christ, in the revelation made to him, prophesied that those who believed in our Christ, would do this for a thousand years in Jerusalem'. It is clear that Justin is reading what was said by the prophets into his interpretation.[1]

The testimony of Irenaeus is interesting. He believed that after the *parousia* Christ would reign on earth for a thousand years, and related that he knew of certain presbyters who had heard St. John say that this was what the Lord Himself had taught. Subsequent writers accepted this interpretation, some expressing doubt about taking the thousand literally, whilst some (who were known as Chiliasts) drew extravagant pictures of the worldly joys of this time. These Chiliastic views naturally provoked a reaction on the part of the orthodox teachers of the Church.

Augustine relates that he also was at first inclined to take the passage literally, but on further study, thought it might refer to the Church. The binding of Satan fulfilled the words of Christ in Mark iii. 27,[2] the thousand years was the period between Christ's first and second coming, the judgment given to the saints was the power of binding and loosing of sins bestowed on the Church, the first resurrection was the spiritual re-birth in baptism.

These ideas reflect the circumstances of Augustine's time, not those of the first century. The martyrs who had shed their blood for the word of God and the testimony of Jesus were for John very real persons. Some of them he had seen and known (he can name Antipas), and whatever else was symbol, *their* resurrection was no less literal for him than that of all the rest of the dead, small and great, after the thousand years.

THE ADVENT AND THE MILLENNIUM

The different views of the time of the Advent in relation to the Millennium have been labelled 'pre-millennial' if the Advent comes before the Millennium, 'post-millennial' if it

[1] See further G. E. Ladd, *The Blessed Hope*, p. 22.
[2] On the meaning of these words see G. E. Ladd, *Crucia. Question. about the Kingdom of God*, pp. 86–88.

comes later, and 'a-millennial' if the Millennium is given a purely 'spiritual' meaning unrelated to the Advent.

a. The post-millennial view takes two forms, one looking upon the thousand years as already past, and the other looking for them in the future. Among the former Aquinas saw the fulfilment of the prophecy in the victory of the Catholic Church commencing with the conversion of Constantine; Hengstenberg saw it in the spread of Christianity from the reign of Charlemagne until the French Revolution. The other form of this view expects to see the fulfilment in a great expansion of the visible Church. In the Victorian period it was sometimes combined with an optimism which looked forward to a gradual upward evolution leading to peace and prosperity, and culminating in the Advent of Christ. Of recent years it has been adopted by some liberals who deny any reality to the Advent other than the continual presence of Christ in the Church.

b. The a-millennial view has defenders among both liberals and conservatives. It is upheld in Swete's commentary, and is ably expounded by W. Hendriksen in *More than Conquerors* and by W. J. Grier in his small book *The Momentous Event*. The upholders of this view agree with Augustine in 'spiritualizing' the 'first resurrection'; and applying the millennial reign, either to the present experience of Christians, or to the reign of the souls of the martyrs and others in heaven.[1]

c. The pre-millennial view takes many different forms, including that known as 'dispensationalism'.[2] Their common element is the belief that Revelation xx should be regarded as prophetic of a period of time *subsequent* to the Advent. To the mind of the present writer this is the only view which does full justice to the text. Although the order of the visions in the Apocalypse may not necessarily denote chronological

[1] See G. E. Ladd, *Crucial Questions about the Kingdom of God*, pp. 143ff.
[2] See *Crucial Questions about the Kingdom of God*, pp. 45, 145ff. Among modern writers who take the pre-millennial view may be mentioned L. S. Chafer, R. A. Ironside and G. Campbell Morgan. Older commentators include Dean Alford and T. Zahn.

sequence, this seems to be the best explanation of the *setting* in which the passage occurs. The marriage of the Lamb has been proclaimed (Rev. xix. 7), and the announcement has been followed by a vision of Christ riding to victory which a majority of expositors identify with the Second Advent. Let it be granted that the number 'a thousand' is symbolical; nevertheless chapter xx presents a number of events as following one another in time. The 'first resurrection' takes place at the beginning of the millennium and that of 'the rest of the dead' at the end; after this there is 'a little season' (verses 3, 7), after which the great final judgment (verses 11–15) and the 'new heavens and the new earth' (chapter xxi).

The expectation of a millennial reign on earth following Christ's return was the prevailing view of the Christian writers of the first three centuries (though there were exceptions), but it was ultimately superseded by that put forward by Augustine (see above, p. 66). Augustine's reference to the Lord's words in Mark iii. 27 is interesting, but those words referred to the time then present, and were not a prediction. The binding of Satan in Revelation xx will be by the hand of an angel, and its purpose is to prevent him from deceiving the nations. He is an optimist of no mean order who imagines that this has been already accomplished. Dr. Kellogg, when the pact that bears his name was signed, declared, 'I am not so blind as to believe that the Millennium has arrived.' And the nations are still deceived.

The crux of the matter is whether the word 'lived' in verse 4 means the same as it does in verse 5. Do both refer to a bodily resurrection or is the former symbolical and the latter literal?

The vision proceeds, 'And I saw the souls of them that were beheaded for the witness of Jesus, and for the word of God' (xx. 4). He had seen them before under the altar where they had been bidden to rest until their number was 'fulfilled' (vi. 9–11). In this vision that time had arrived, and now 'they lived and reigned with Christ a thousand years. . . . This is the first resurrection' (xx. 4, 5). Here interpretations differ widely.

Augustine saw in it a reference to Christian baptism; but whatever it may *typify*, that cannot possibly be what it meant to John, or to those to whom he wrote. Those who had been beheaded were men, like Antipas, whom they had known. Their conversion and baptism were long past. Their souls had lain under God's altar crying for vengeance; now they were to live again. 'The opening statement of verse 5 shows with all the clarity desired that *the first resurrection* is a literal resurrection from the dead, not a synonym for the new birth.'[1]

Besides the souls of the martyrs, others enter into John's vision, namely, confessors who had resisted all temptation to emperor worship. He does not say whether these are dead or living, but together with the martyrs 'they lived and reigned'. They are distinguished from 'the rest of the dead', who 'lived not again until the thousand years were finished'. These words point to a literal resurrection. They who 'have part in the first resurrection' (a limited number) are 'blessed and holy' and they 'cannot be hurt of the second death'. Our Lord used words which point in the same direction when, in controversy with the Sadducees, He referred to those 'which shall be accounted worthy to obtain that world, and the resurrection from the dead' (Lk. xx. 35). This implies that 'some from among the dead are raised, while others as yet are not'.[2]

This description of 'the first resurrection' in Revelation xx invites comparison also with 1 Corinthians xv, the great revelation concerning the resurrection committed to St. Paul. This reads, 'Every man in his own order: Christ the firstfruits; afterward they that are Christ's at his coming. Then cometh the end . . .' (1 Cor. xv. 23, 24). The word 'order' (verse 23) does not in itself refer to time, but means 'rank', and is so used of ranks in an army. Three such ranks are involved, first in a rank by Himself is Christ, risen from the dead already, as a kind of firstfruit; then, after a lapse of time, those that are

---

[1] G. R. Beasley-Murray, *The New Bible Commentary*, p. 1195. Dean Alford is even more emphatic that this is the only legitimate interpretation.

[2] Plummer, *I.C.C.*, *in loc.*

Christ's at His coming (*parousia*). Then, after a further lapse of time, the end. No further resurrection is stated, but it is implied, for all those of a third rank. The correspondence with Revelation xx is striking, as also with 1 Thessalonians iv.[1]

A similar distinction is made by Paul in Philippians iii. 11 where he expresses the hope that he may 'attain unto the resurrection from the dead' (RV). The double use in the Greek of the particle *ek*, 'from', emphasizes the difference between this and 'the general resurrection of the dead, whether good or bad'.[2] Compare Romans i. 4.

John says that the martyrs and confessors 'lived and reigned' with Christ a thousand years. This is a prospect so glorious as to make us eager to know whether we may share in it, and perhaps soon. We turn back to Revelation v. 9, 10, where the twenty-four elders sing a new song proclaiming that those whom Christ has redeemed 'reign upon the earth' already.[3] Surely therefore we shall share His reign, whether on earth or in heaven, when He comes again. This was promised to the overcomers in Laodicea (Rev. iii. 21), and may be ours if we overcome in these Laodicean times. 'It is a faithful saying: For if we be dead with him, we shall also live with him: If we suffer, we shall also reign with him' (2 Tim. ii. 11, 12).

DISPENSATIONALISM

New problems are raised by the system of interpretation known as 'dispensationalism'. As we have already seen, this view divides the history of mankind into a number of eras, or dispensations, in each of which God dispenses justice upon a principle specially belonging to that period.[4] The dispensation of 'law' beginning with Moses, was followed by the dispensation of grace, instituted by Jesus Christ (Rom. vi. 14f.),

---

[1] A passage in the Didache reads, 'Then shall the world see the Lord coming upon the clouds of heaven, and the resurrection of the dead, but not all.'

[2] Lightfoot, *in loc.*

[3] Note the present tense in RV.

[4] See L. S. Chafer, *Dispensationalism* (Dallas, 1951).

and so far all will agree. But difference of opinion arises concerning the further teaching that at the *parousia* the present 'church age' will be succeeded by a 'kingdom age', namely the Millennium, when the Old Testament promises to Israel will receive a literal fulfilment. It is said that Christ will set up the throne of David in Jerusalem and reign over a restored and converted Israel for a literal thousand years. But the throne of David receives no mention in Revelation xx, nor is there anything to imply a limitation of reference to Jews. The site where Gog and Magog are destroyed is, however, 'the camp of the saints' and 'the beloved city' (Rev. xx. 9).

THE PROMISES TO ISRAEL

Recent events have brought the state of Israel into the centre of the political picture, and have created a renewed interest in the Old Testament prophecies to Israel. Certainly the Jews have had a remarkable history. Their dispersion, their sufferings and the persecution they have endured, and in spite of this, their preservation as a racial entity, may well be regarded as the fulfilment of prophecy. It is said that when Frederick the Great asked his chaplain for a proof of the truth of Christianity, he received the reply, 'The Jews, your majesty!'

When the Balfour Declaration was issued during the First World War, promising the Jews a 'national home' in Palestine, and when that promise was afterwards fulfilled under the British mandate, many Christian people saw in these events the fulfilment of the Old Testament prophecies of the re-gathering of dispersed Israel to the land of promise. It is when we come to consider the promises in detail, one by one, that the problem is seen to be complex. The original promise to Abraham, and renewed to Isaac and Jacob, of a numerous seed and a land to dwell in, was certainly fulfilled. Joshua said truly, 'not one thing hath failed' (Jos. xxiii. 14). But immediately he threatened that the Lord would destroy them from off the land if they transgressed, and served other gods. The promises were therefore conditional. The promise to Solomon upon the building of the temple could equally be revoked should they prove unfaithful (1 Ki. ix. 4–7). And in later times the prophets, despairing of the people as a whole, limited the promises to a faithful 'remnant' (see Is. x. 22; Je. xxiii. 3; Rom. ix. 27).

The problem becomes further complicated as we turn to the New Testament and find some of the old promises extended to include Gentile as well as Jewish believers (see Rom. ii. 9–12; Gal. iii. 22, 28f.). This has led many scholars to refer to the Church the blessings which were promised to Israel in the Old Testament. Let the reader compare the headings of pages and chapters in the AV with those provided in the Scofield Bible, and he will find that many prophecies which the latter refers to a restored Israel in the yet future 'kingdom age' are, in the AV, applied to the Church.[1]

It could fairly be said that Paul himself found the problem difficult as he grappled with it in Romans ix–xi.[2] He is sure that none of God's promises will fail (and so are we); and he loves to look forward to a time when the fullness of the Gentiles is come in, 'and so all Israel shall be saved' (Rom. xi. 25, 26). The latter words might mean either the elect of Israel, those whom 'God foreknew' (so Origen), or the Israel of God, both Jew and Gentile (Calvin)[3] or a national conversion (Sanday and Headlam).

To connect the words with the Millennium is hazardous, for Paul does not mention the Advent, or the Davidic kingdom. But we need not wait for the Millennium; we can, and must, take note of our present duty. This is, here and now, to feel gratitude to the Jewish race through whom the revelation of God has come to us, to seek their conversion, and to welcome them into fellowship. This is the more incumbent upon us today, to make some amends for the wicked treatment meted out to them, which has brought

---

[1] See further A. M. Stibbs, *God's Church* (I.V.F., 1959), pp. 51–59.

[2] For a careful exposition of these chapters see P. E. Hughes, *The Divine Plan for Jew and Gentile* (Tyndale Press, 1951).

[3] See A. M. Stibbs, *God's Church*, pp. 51–59.

shame and reproach on the Christian name. The 'fulness of the Gentiles' and the salvation of Israel are closely bound together (Rom. xi. 25, 28).

But, it may well be asked, was not the *land* promised to the Jews, and is not their return to it the fulfilment of prophecy? The land of Canaan was indeed promised to Abraham and that promise was fulfilled under Joshua. But they rebelled against Jehovah, and defiled His land, and it was taken from them (Je. xvi. 18; Lk. xx. 16). Who then are the rightful heirs of the land today?

Once again, the answer is far from simple. Is it a mere matter of natural descent? If so, did the twelve apostles and their followers forfeit their birthright by becoming 'Christians'? And what of their descendants? There are families in Palestine today whose ancestors go back to those early Christians, and who have never left the land of their fathers; some belong to the Greek church, some have become Moslems, others have become Roman Catholic or Protestant. When the writer was in Palestine between the wars, he met one of the latter in Nazareth who put to him the question, 'Is it my duty to give up my piece of land which has been in my family for centuries, to a Jewish immigrant from Eastern Europe?' What is the answer?

The problem of race or faith has again assumed prominence in the endeavour of the Israel Government to answer the question, Who is a Jew? The definition adopted is, 'Anyone who in good faith considers himself to be a Jew, and who does not profess any other religion'. So the Jew who becomes a Christian today forfeits his rights as a Jew.

CONCLUSION

As to what follows the Advent, both the brevity and the mystery of the prophecy of the thousand years discourage speculation, but provide an incentive to faithful witness and a ground for hope. Jesus will come to reign; those blessed and holy ones who share in the first resurrection will reign with

Him. So, being justified by faith, 'we rejoice in hope of the glory of God' (Rom. v. 1, 2). And, for poor sinners who are sorely tried by the fiery darts of Satan, it is no small comfort to know that he will be bound, and unable to deceive.

Having regard to the Old Testament promises to Israel, and to the belief of many that they may forecast a great turning to God of the Jews now returning to the land, we do well to watch and pray. We have encouragement to observe 'the signs of the times', and if we see in them a prelude to our Lord's return, we may well lift up our hearts and rejoice.

CHAPTER VII

THE ENEMY

IT is never wise to underestimate the strength of the forces ranged against you. In answer to the disciples' question, 'When?', the Lord's first word was, 'Take heed . . .' (Mk. xiii. 5), and this is a sign of its prime importance. He went on to tell them of evil days ahead, opposition and persecution, and a veritable campaign of falsehood. Foreseeing this, He said, 'Take heed lest any man deceive you.' There is no word in the Greek corresponding to 'man'. The reference is perfectly general; it might include both 'false Christs' and 'seducing spirits' and Satan himself.

Events proved the need for this warning. Opposition was followed by persecution, false Christs·arose and many were deceived. Years afterwards Paul repeated the warning when writing to Timothy. 'Now the Spirit speaketh expressly, that in the latter times some shall depart from the faith, giving heed to seducing spirits, and doctrines of devils' (1 Tim. iv. 1). He had previously advised the Corinthians to be aware of Satan's devices (2 Cor. ii. 11). In his second letter to Timothy he again says 'that in the last days perilous times shall come' (2 Tim. iii. 1; cf. 2 Tim. iv. 3).

Persecution of the Christian Church had gone still further when John wrote his first Epistle, saying, 'Little children, it is the last time: and as ye have heard that antichrist shall come, even now are there many antichrists; whereby we know that it is the last time' (1 Jn. ii. 18).

Were these sayings intended only for the persecuted Christians of the first century, or have they a message for us? At the close of the nineteenth century many thought that the advance of science was leading on to a golden age; today men are afraid lest it lead us to mutual destruction. After the First World War, many thought the League of Nations was a guarantee of peace; but war broke out again. There is still need to 'take heed'.

THE GREAT DECEPTION

There are many who deny the existence of Satan; they are grossly deceived. Paul taught the Corinthians that it was no wonder that there were false apostles when Satan could 'fashion himself into an angel of light' (2 Cor. xi. 13, 14, RV).

Recurring revolutions in the East of recent times have made us familiar with their technique; the revolutionaries put on a fair face, and pose as the friends of everybody until their deep-laid plots are complete. They conceal their identity until the time is ripe, and then strike a sudden blow, and seize the power.

C. S. Lewis, in his book, *The Screwtape Letters*, has taught the present generation how Satan employs a similar technique to deceive young Christians into complacency, and an assumption of inspired intelligence in denying his existence.

The god of this age is still at work, blinding the eyes of unbelievers (2 Cor. iv. 4). Jesus was not deceived; there can be no reasonable doubt that He believed in a personal devil. The story of the Temptation bears on its face the marks of authenticity; it can only have originated in Jesus Himself. The same is true of His sayings, some of which are quoted below, which are too many and too striking to be set aside by any critical device. He felt the full force of Satan's temptation and resisted; and those who similarly resist will be equally convinced of Satan's reality.

For this reason, as the last days draw near, the Christian student should not grudge some time for seeking what light the Bible can throw upon the enemy and his tactics, and in particular what Jesus Himself has to say.

THE ENEMY

The Bible consistently pictures Satan as the enemy of God, of the human race, and, above all, of Christ, the Son of God.

The sad story begins in the garden of Eden where he launches his subtle attack by casting doubt upon God's word, a method he has used up to the present day. Having caught Adam and Eve in his trap, his doom is pronounced, but it is foretold that he shall bruise 'the heel' of the woman's seed (Gn. iii. 15). He persecuted Job, and the book shows how easily philosophy may go astray over the meaning and purpose of the afflictions of the righteous. It also shows that the devil's power is limited and that he who endures to the end will be saved. Passing over the other Scriptures, let us come to the Gospels. Satan cannot hide his existence from Jesus, and knows it would be vain to challenge the written word; he therefore quotes it, but distorts and misapplies its meaning. This is a trick he still plays upon the simple. But in Jesus he found One stronger than he; he was rebuffed and retreated.

Let us note how Jesus describes him. He is like a strong man armed, who encounters one stronger than himself (Mk. iii. 27). Or he is like the birds of the air picking up seed; no sooner is the good seed, the word of God, sown in man's hearts, than Satan swoops down, 'and taketh away the word' (Mk. iv. 15). He is 'the enemy' of the Son of man, for when He sows in His field good seed, the children of the kingdom, the devil, in imitation, sows 'the children of the wicked one' (Mt. xiii. 37–39). He works his mischief while men sleep. He tempted Peter to folly (Mk. viii. 32, 33), and would, if he could, have sifted him like wheat (Lk. xxii. 31). In later years Peter described him as a roaring lion (1 Pet. v. 8). Satan is 'a murderer from the beginning . . . a liar, and the father of it' (Jn. viii. 44). Satan is 'the prince of this world', the 'world' which Jesus overcame, but when Jesus was lifted up on the cross, judgment was given, and he was cast out (Jn. xii. 31–33). Can we wonder at the emphasis Jesus laid upon the necessity to 'take heed'?

John tells us that the Son of God was manifested 'that he might destroy the works of the devil'. Satan's kingdom began to fall when power was granted to the disciples to cast out devils (Lk. x. 18), and when Jesus loosed one whom Satan had bound with a spirit of infirmity (Lk. xiii. 11, 16). He received his heaviest blow at Calvary, but he is not yet dead.

The existence of Satan received public acknowledgment when war was raging; it is somewhat camouflaged in times of peace. Let us not be deceived; 'he that committeth sin is of the devil' (1 Jn. iii. 8), and we can see him at work all around us—and within. Whether Satan goes about 'as a roaring lion' (1 Pet. v. 8) or poses as 'an angel of light' (2 Cor. xi. 14), the fight still goes on.

In his concordance Alexander Cruden begins the list of references to the 'devil' thus; 'He is a most wicked angel, the implacable enemy and tempter of the human race, especially believers, whom he desires to devour (1 Pet. v. 8)'. His list of references, beginning with Matthew iv. 1 and ending with Revelation xx. 10, fully supports this description.

THE WARFARE

In a well-known passage (Eph. vi. 11-16) Paul describes the life of the Christian as a wrestling with the 'spiritual hosts of wickedness' (RV). The evil one casts his fiery darts against the Christian, who quenches them with the shield of faith. In the book of Revelation the reader 'sees a picture of the conflict between God and the devil, between good and evil, the great forces of the world, the flesh and the devil, brought to bear on the Christian Church, and the Church finally triumphant in Christ'.[1]

On earth, so Ephesians vi. 11 tells us, it is a warfare of deception; but it is revealed as proceeding from a 'war in heaven' (Rev. xii. 7). In chapter xii John sees a woman clothed with the sun, symbol for the Church,[2] and she brings forth a Son, who is shown by the description to be Christ. Against them a great red dragon makes war, but in vain. The woman is protected; her Son is taken up to the throne of God. The war in heaven results in the dragon being cast down to

---

[1] B. F. C. Atkinson, *The War in Heaven*, p. 5.

[2] 'The mystical mother of the Lord . . . is the Jewish Church' (Swete).

earth, 'having great wrath, because he knoweth that he hath but a short time' (Rev. xii. 12). It is a warfare in which there is no release; and its intensity grows greater as the revelation progresses. In chapter xiii, two agents of Satan are revealed as the beast and the false prophet. Doubtless in John's mind these represented the Roman power in its civil and its religious aspects. But they may, and most interpreters think that they do, pre-figure forces of evil as the end of the age approaches.

In Revelation xvi we seem to reach a point where the Advent is near. Evil spirits from the dragon's mouth go forth to gather the kings of the earth 'to the battle of that great day of God Almighty' (xvi. 14). Unexpectedly a voice breaks in, 'Behold, I come as a thief'; and we have no doubt as to the speaker. This is followed by the words, 'And he gathered them together into a place called in the Hebrew tongue Armageddon' (xvi. 16). The picture is of a battle taking place at the Mountain of Megiddo in the north of Palestine, the place where Barak overthrew Sisera and where King Josiah met his death (Jdg. v. 19; 2 Ki. xxiii. 29).

John does not describe the battle further, or record its result; but turns aside to describe the pouring out of the seventh vial. The voice of Jesus in verse 15 associates the battle with the Second Advent, and many commentators look for a literal fulfilment in Northern Palestine. Armageddon has become a popular synonym for a war at the end of the age. This may prove to be so; but it also may be that the apostle is only using a picture to show how the kings of the earth may one day come under the judgment of God Almighty.

In chapter xix there is a second picture of a battle; here Christ, followed by the armies in heaven, engages 'the beast, and the kings of the earth, and their armies' (xix. 19); they are overcome and cast into the lake of fire. The account is crowded with metaphor, and it is not easy to say where symbol ends and reality begins; but the victory seems to synchronize with the return of Christ in glory. If this be a prediction, who are we to understand by the 'beast'? Will there arise a personal antichrist?

THE 'MAN OF SIN'

Before attempting any answer to this question, let us turn to the picture of the 'man of sin',[1] the opposing power so named by Paul in 2 Thessalonians ii. 3. Paul writes about 'the coming of our Lord Jesus Christ, and . . . our gathering together unto him', and he warns his readers that the day of the Lord will not arrive until there come first 'the apostasy' (*apostasis*, 'rebellion', or 'falling away'), and the 'man of sin' be revealed; and this will not happen until 'he who now hinders be removed' (verses 1–7).

Irenaeus and other second-century writers thought that the reference was to a future, personal antichrist and that Rome was the restraining power. Cyril of Jerusalem connected this passage with the prophecies of Daniel ii and vii. He expected the Roman Empire, the fourth kingdom of these visions, to break up into ten smaller kingdoms, when antichrist would appear, and the Advent then follow.

In the days of the Reformation it was common to identify the 'man of sin' with the papal power. Alford comments thus: 'It cannot be doubted, there are many and striking points of correspondence with the language of the prophecy in the acts and professions of those who have successively had that power.' How many readers of the Authorized Version have observed a little sentence in the Dedication referring to this? King James is praised for his zeal in 'writing in defence of the Truth, (which hath given such a blow unto that man of sin, as will not be healed,)'. Fewer still will be aware of the fact that King James wrote and published a treatise demonstrating that the papacy is the 'man of sin', which accounts for the praise accorded to him, and shows how widely this belief was then accepted. It is still held by many, and must be accorded due respect.

But if not the papacy, shall we see a world dictator arise among the communists, who will fulfil the role? Their opposition to Christianity is avowed, and their methods

[1] Some MSS read 'lawlessness'.

Satanic. While this book was being written the author listened to one who had been sentenced to ten months in prison for the crime of attempting to gather a group of young people for Bible study. This commenced with many days of the diabolical torture of 'questioning' which, day after day, commenced in the early morning and went on until late at night. But whether antichrist arise from the ranks of the professing Church or elsewhere, it is vain to speculate; the mystery of iniquity may be even now working beneath the surface (2 Thes. ii. 7) and leading to a new apostasy. Let us therefore study the Scriptures, and watch, and pray.

In his Epistles John described the apostates of his times as 'antichrists' (1 Jn. ii. 18f., 2 Jn. 7). In the Revelation he uses the symbol of a beast (xiii. 11–17) to picture a great blasphemer, inspired by Satan to persecute the Church as the Advent approaches. The same was prefigured in the book of Daniel; and in both books the ominous period of 1,260 days is found.[1] Much labour has been bestowed, and not a little difference of opinion has arisen, in the endeavour to find a literal interpretation of this figure of the antichrist and the mystic period of three and a half years, into the detail of which we cannot enter here. They combine, nevertheless, to warn us of the existence of an enemy strong and powerful in that old serpent, the devil. And he is not dead yet, though he would like us to think so.

THE ASSURANCE OF VICTORY

Whatever else may seem obscure in the prophecies of the end of the age, they unanimously declare that the day is coming when all the powers of evil will be destroyed. As John puts it, 'for this purpose the Son of God was manifested, that he might destroy the works of the devil' (1 Jn. iii. 8). These works are manifest enough all around us. We have seen them in the horrid cruelties of total warfare, in the hatred of Christianity manifested in China, and the many ways in which 'the god of

---

[1] See Dn. vii. 25, xii. 7; Rev. xi. 2, 3, xii. 4, 6, 14, xiii. 5.

this world hath blinded the minds of them which believe not (2 Cor. iv. 4).

But how and when will they be destroyed? In part now, when the light of the gospel drives the darkness from the hearts of men, and when the Son of God is manifested in the heart of the believer. Already Christ's faithful witnesses gain the victory 'by the blood of the Lamb, and by the word of their testimony' (Rev. xii. 11), but soon the victory will be complete.

Jesus will come again. He died on the cross that 'through death he might bring to nought him that had the power of death, that is, the devil' (Heb. ii. 14, RV). At His coming the man of sin will be destroyed, as it were in a flash (2 Thes. ii. 8). Death, the last enemy, 'will be swallowed up in victory' (1 Cor. xv. 54–57). Then death, and Hades, and Satan himself will be cast into the fire. Then will be seen new heavens and a new earth.

The victory of Christ is sure and His victory will be ours. Therefore, 'be ye stedfast, unmoveable, always abounding in the work of the Lord, forasmuch as ye know that your labour is not in vain in the Lord' (1 Cor. xv. 58).

CHAPTER VIII

JUDGMENT AND SALVATION

GENERATION after generation, from the second century to the present time, Christians have recited the words of the Apostles' Creed, 'From thence He shall come to judge the quick and the dead.' The reader may have repeated those words scores, even hundreds of times, as one of the essentials of the Christian faith. It will therefore be no waste of time to give them a little careful consideration.

Bishop Pearson, in his classic treatise on the Creed, observes that here we have four facts stated: (a) Jesus Christ shall come; (b) He shall come 'thence', that is, from where He is now seated at the right hand of God the Father; (c) He will come 'to judge', and (d) those whom He will judge will include both 'the living and the dead'. Each of these statements is supported in his book by abundant quotations from Scripture. So the Creed links together the Advent and the Judgment.

The expectation of a future judgment is not peculiar to Christianity; it agrees with the witness of our conscience and our sense of moral responsibility. It is involved in the belief that God is the Creator and moral ruler of the universe; it helps to explain and compensate for the inequalities of life, and has been held by philosophers in many lands and in all ages. But it is only Christians who believe that Jesus Christ will be the Judge; and how wonderful this is! From the fifth century they have sung in the Te Deum, 'We believe that Thou shalt come to be our Judge. We therefore pray Thee, help Thy servants, whom Thou hast redeemed with Thy precious blood.'

The Creed has also incorporated the further truth that, when Christ comes to judge, there will be a generation of men then living. In the third century some writers interpreted the words 'the quick and the dead' as they occur in Scripture as meaning those who are alive or dead spiritually. Augustine said that he had frequently pondered over this question, but every time had come back to the decision that the words must be taken in their literal sense. The simple words of the Creed rest upon the justice of God, which is proclaimed in the whole Bible from the story of the Fall to the book of Revelation.

It is good news for poor sinners that God the Father has 'committed all judgment unto the Son' (Jn. v. 22), because this means that He who will come to be our Judge, has already come to be our Saviour. Peter fully realized this when, in the house of Cornelius, he bore his witness to the resurrection of Jesus Christ, and testified that 'it is he which was ordained of God to be the Judge of quick and dead'; and lest terror should fall upon his hearers, he added, 'To him give all the prophets witness, that through his name whosoever believeth in him shall receive remission of sins' (Acts x. 42, 43; cf. Acts xvii. 31; 1 Pet. iv. 5).

In writing to Timothy, Paul uses the same truth as a ground for urgency in preaching the word (2 Tim. iv. 1, 2); and early in the second century we read in the writings of Polycarp, 'who shall come as the judge of the living and the dead'.[1]

THE SALVATION-STORY

We see, then, that there is certainly a judgment to come. But God's judgment is not only future; the Bible is a record of divine judgment from Genesis to Revelation.[2] In the garden of Eden He pronounced judgment upon Adam and Eve and drove them out of Eden; His judgment fell upon the wickedness of the men of Sodom; it fell upon Jerusalem and it fell upon Babylon. Nevertheless, German scholars have truly named the Bible *Heilsgeschichte*, 'the Salvation-story', and such it is. For whilst judgment is a necessary adjunct of God's justice, the salvation of mankind is God's age-long plan. The

[1] *Epistle to the Philippians*, II.
[2] The Bible usage of the words 'judge' and 'judgment' provides a wide field for study.

Lamb was slain from the foundation of the world (Rev. xiii. 8).
Nor is there any contradiction, for in the Bible judgment and
salvation are closely linked together as the obverse and reverse
of one coin. So when God pronounced judgment upon Eve,
at the same time He promised her a seed who should bruise
the serpent's head. After the Flood, God made a covenant of
grace with Noah. This is also the moral of the book of Judges.
It relates how, time and again, the children of Israel sinned
against the Lord and He delivered them into the hands of their
enemies. But when they repented and cried unto Him, He
heard them and raised up for them a 'saviour' (Jdg. iii. 9, 15,
RV), who then became their 'judge'. So mercy and judgment
are bound up together (Ps. ci. 1); but 'mercy rejoiceth against
judgment' (Jas. ii. 13).

In the Old Testament the divine judgment is seen in a series
of acts in the course of human history whereby individual and
national sin is punished, or the righteous vindicated. 'God is
the judge; he putteth down one, and setteth up another'
(Ps. lxxv. 7). This thought of judgment as a historical process
is continued into the New Testament. Judgment will fall upon
Jerusalem (Lk. xix. 43f.), and continue to the seven last
plagues (Rev. xv. 1). Yet all the time 'God so loved the world,
that he gave his only begotten Son, that whosoever believeth
in him should not perish, but have everlasting life' (Jn. iii. 16).
The judgment therefore *includes* salvation. So the Creed might
have run, 'Thence He shall come again to gather His elect'.

When the Son of God was born into the world, a new stage
was reached; He was given the name of Saviour ('Jesus'), and
a new criterion of judgment was set up, namely that of
personal faith in Him. Whosoever believeth on Him shall
have eternal life, but 'he that believeth not is condemned
already' (Jn. iii. 16, 18). Moreover, while the divine judgments
continue to be manifested in history, there is a new emphasis
upon a judgment which is still future (Mt. xii. 41f.); as Paul
says, a 'day when God shall judge the secrets of men by Jesus
Christ according to my gospel' (Rom. ii. 16). When Jesus was
lifted up on the cross, it was judgment for the 'world', but

salvation for all who should look to Him with the eye of faith (Jn. xii. 31). Henceforth, 'it is appointed unto men once to die, but after this the judgment: so Christ was once offered to bear the sins of many; and unto them that look for him shall he appear the second time without sin unto salvation' (Heb. ix. 27, 28). Thus, salvation has the last word.

ADVENT AND JUDGMENT

When we repeat 'From thence He shall come to judge the quick and the dead', we connect the 'judgment' with the 'coming', and with the resurrection. Let us therefore enquire next how our Lord Himself dealt with these connections.

a. Let us go back first to the Mount of Olives, as our Lord announces His return (Mk. xiii. 24–27). There is no explicit mention either of 'judgment' or of 'resurrection'. Yet the gathering of the 'elect' implies a division among men, and suggests the possibility of the resurrection of believers. In these respects it corresponds closely with Paul's teaching in 1 Corinthians xv. 25 and 1 Thessalonians iv. 15–17, in both of which, however, the resurrection of believers is quite explicit.

b. In Matthew xxv the discourse is continued by the addition of two parables. That of the ten virgins inculcates the need of spiritual preparedness, that of the talents the fullest use of the present opportunity, in view of the Lord's return. These lead up to a great judgment scene, in which the Son of man sits on the throne of His glory, and before Him are gathered the nations, and He shall separate them one from another, as a shepherd divideth the sheep from the goats (Mt. xxv. 31ff.). Here judgment is in the foreground, the Advent has receded into the background, the Son of man is not seen in the clouds, but seated on His throne. The judgment is individual, not national; 'all nations' should not be limited to the Gentiles; and the Lord's 'brethren' may be His disciples, or indeed any who stand in need of help (cf. Mt. xii. 50).

Whilst the picture is that of a general judgment, the lesson involved must be related to the setting of the words, and the circumstances in which they were spoken. The four disciples would soon find themselves without their Master, sent forth as His ambassadors and representatives unto the world; it is essential that they should be possessed by His Spirit. The terms He uses here are similar to those in which He described His own ministry at its outset (Lk. iv. 18; Is. lvi. 1f.). Unless they should be possessed by the Spirit of Christ, they could be none of His (Rom. viii. 9). There is room here for much heart-searching.

c. In the earlier part of His ministry the Lord pictures the final judgment in the parables of the wheat and tares, and of the drawnet into which were gathered fish, both good and bad (Mt. xiii. 24–30, 36–43, 47–50). The Lord divides men into two classes, the 'children of the kingdom', and the 'children of the wicked one'. The difference may not be visible now, but they are in absolute contrast in both their nature and origin. Their character will be manifested and their destiny sealed at 'the end of the age' (RV mg., see below).

From the earliest times these parables have been applied to members of the visible Church, some true and some false. Resurrection is not mentioned, nor the Advent; they are not necessary to the lesson involved.

d. Two sayings of the Lord may be considered here, which connect resurrection with judgment.

(i) In John v. 22–29, Jesus was talking with 'the Jews' after the healing at Bethesda. He claimed that the Father had committed all judgment to the Son (22), and that those who heard His word and believed, should 'not come into condemnation' (24). Even at the time He spake, dead souls were gaining this life (25); but there was a future time coming when 'all that are in the tombs shall hear his voice, and shall come forth; they that have done good, unto the resurrection of life; and they that have done ill, unto the resurrection of judgment' (28, 29, RV).

(ii) In Luke xx. 35, when answering the question of the Sadducees concerning 'the resurrection', He said, 'they that are accounted worthy to attain to that world (age), and the resurrection from the dead, neither marry, nor are given in marriage' (RV). In the Greek the preposition *ek*, 'out' or 'from', is prefixed to the word resurrection; thus suggesting that the resurrection is selective and not complete.

THE TWO AGES

It is important that we should understand aright the conception of the two ages,[1] which lies behind some of these sayings, and others in the New Testament. The Greek word *aiōn* (AV, 'world', RV or RV mg., 'age') must be carefully distinguished from *kosmos* (AV and RV, 'world'). This latter is the 'world' of men or of nature, as it appeared to Greek thought as an ordered whole, and extended to the whole universe (hence our word 'cosmic'). This is the 'world' which Jesus came to save (Jn. xii. 46) but which proved to be hostile to Him (1 Jn. iii. 13).

But the word *aiōn* is based upon the idea of two (or more)[2] 'ages' or periods of time, each of which possesses its own specific character as a mode of existence. Therefore when Jesus said that 'the harvest is the end of the world (age)', He did not mean the destruction of the globe on which we live, but the consummation of our present mode of existence, after which a new age with new conditions would supervene.[3] Jesus promised His continuing presence with His disciples so long as the present age shall endure (Mt. xxviii. 20).

Paul says that Jesus Christ gave Himself for our sins that He might 'deliver us from this present evil age' (Gal. i. 4), over which Satan rules as a god (2 Cor. iv. 4). Those who attain to

---

[1] For the use of this idea in Scripture, see G. E. Ladd, *Crucial Questions about the Kingdom of God*, pp. 167f. For the difference between its use in Scripture and in Jewish apocalypses see articles by G. E. Ladd in *The Evangelical Quarterly* for April and July 1958.

[2] Cf. 1 Cor. x. 11, RV.

[3] For examples of the meaning and use of the word *aiōn* in various contexts, see Dalman, *The Words of Jesus* (T. and T. Clark, Edinburgh, 1909), pp. 147–156.

that age will find everything different (Lk. xx. 35); and already Christians have begun to taste something of its powers (Heb. vi. 5). With our Lord's *parousia*, the new age will begin (Mt. xxiv. 3), we shall be changed and we shall see clearly things which now are only dimly discerned (1 Cor. xiii. 9). Life eternal belongs to the coming age (Mk. x. 30), but it is already ours (Jn. v. 24). This new era, like our present age, may consist of many stages. One standing on the ridge at Simla and looking out over the broad Indus plain, sees the snowy Himalayas like a single white ribbon stretched across the horizon. Yet, on a nearer approach, it is found that one range stretches beyond another, and as each height is reached, others lie beyond.

ONE JUDGMENT OR MORE

We soon find that there is a wide variety in the ways in which the future judgment of mankind is described in the New Testament. While this helps to impress upon us its certainty, and our need to guide our actions in the light of it, it makes it difficult to combine them into one single picture. But is this necessary? It is nowhere stated that the new heaven and the new earth will be created simultaneously with Christ's return in the clouds, and some Scriptures imply the contrary.[1] The present age has gone through many stages; it may be the same in the age to come.

It is possible to collect most of the various statements into three groups according to the aspects of the Advent and of the judgment which they set forth. (a) Some declare the salvation of God's elect, (b) some foretell the judgment of the works of Christians, and (c) some refer to the great final judgment of all mankind.

a. There are three passages which describe the Lord's coming in simple, concrete terms free from symbol or parable, namely, the words of Christ in Mark xiii. 26f., the 'word of the Lord' given to Paul in 1 Thessalonians iv. 15–17, and his statement that 'they that are Christ's' will be raised 'at his

[1] See above, pp. 66f.

coming (*parousia*)' (1 Cor. xv. 23)[1] All three alike deal only with Christ's followers, and describe what happens to them at the time of Christ's coming. There is no mention of 'judgment', but they describe a severance between those who belong to Christ and those who do not, which involves judgment. See also Philippians iii. 20, 21.

b. On two occasions Paul makes use of the simile of the 'judgment seat', or raised platform used by Roman magistrates. He rebukes those who would judge or look down upon their brethren, 'for we shall all stand before the judgement-seat of God' (Rom. xiv. 10, RV). Man is not the judge of his fellowmen, but God is the judge of all. The lesson to be learned is found in verse 13.

The other occasion is when he is writing to the Corinthians and looking forward to being present with the Lord, to whom he longs to render acceptable service, 'for we must all appear before the judgment seat of Christ' (2 Cor. v. 10). For this reason, because he knows that all men will so stand, he is the more earnest in his efforts to persuade men (2 Cor. v. 11). He is not expressing any doubt of his own salvation, but his sense of increased responsibility because Christ, his Saviour whom he loves to serve, will one day be his Judge. In addition there are passages which speak of rewards for disciples, of which some connect the giving of these with the *parousia*, such as Luke xix. 17, 19; 1 Corinthians iii. 9–13; Revelation xxii. 12. There will be joy for all Christians, but not dead uniformity in the age to come.

c. A third class are passages such as the parables of the tares and the drawnet, the separation of the sheep and goats, the resurrection as foretold in John v. 28f., and the dread scene before the great white throne of God in Revelation xx. 11–15, in which those who are saved enter into eternal life, whilst those who are lost receive 'eternal punishment'.[2] The wrath

---

[1] See G. E. Ladd, *Crucial Questions about the Kingdom of God*, p. 178.

[2] Yet in that wonderful book this is quickly followed by the words, 'I will give unto him that is athirst of the fountain of the water of life freely' (Rev. xxi. 6).

of God is a terrible reality, which, Paul tells us, 'is revealed from heaven against all ungodliness and unrighteousness of men' (Rom. i. 18); but he exhorts his converts to wait for the Son of God from heaven, because He has delivered them 'from the wrath to come' (1 Thes. i. 10). The 'day of salvation' (2 Cor. vi. 2) has lasted nearly two thousand years; the 'day of judgment' cannot be cramped into twenty-four hours.

When and how God will accomplish these judgments it is perhaps not necessary for us to know. If the thousand years of Revelation xx be more than a meaningless symbol there will be some interval between the moment when Christ will be seen coming in the clouds, and the final judgment of mankind. Whatever may intervene between the *parousia* and that judgment, one thing is clear. Those who belong to Christ will, at His coming, be gathered to Him for ever (1 Thes. iv. 17). For them there is 'no condemnation' (Rom. viii. 1); it will not be theirs to stand before the great white throne. For them it is enough to 'make their calling and election sure' by living the Christian life (2 Pet. i. 5–11), to use the thought of judgment as an incentive to more earnest evangelism (2 Tim. iv. 1–3), and to put into practice all the other lessons in the Scriptures we have been considering.

Some find a difficulty in reconciling the various *standards of judgment* set before us. Will a man be (here note the present tense) judged by his 'work' (1 Pet. i. 7, but note 1 Pet. i. 4), or by his treatment of others (Mt. xxv. 45), or by every 'idle word' (Mt. xii. 36, 37)? What then becomes of justification by faith? The difficulty is superficial; it will be greatly lessened as each reference is considered in its context with the help of a good commentary. After all, what standard of judgment is there except a man's life? and life is made up of words and deeds. But salvation by faith supervenes to avert judgment (Rom. iii. 20–28); and unto them that look for Him Christ will appear the second time 'without sin unto salvation' (Heb. ix. 28).

Should any reader still be overcome by fear, perhaps a personal testimony may be helpful. The writer cannot forget a day in Cambridge many years ago, and the shock experienced as some friends told him how another undergraduate, a freshman like himself, had been struck dead by lightning while crossing Midsummer Common on his way to the May races. The thought rushed into his mind, 'Supposing I had been in his place. Where should I stand in the judgment?' Trying to find a true answer, John v. 24 came to mind. 'Yes. I have heard and accepted the word of Jesus; and I have believed on God who sent Him. So then, I shall not come into condemnation; my sins are blotted out; I have passed from death unto life.' The fear of death and judgment was taken away, and has not returned.

In the year 1738 John Wesley preached a sermon at the Bedford assizes before the assembled judges, sheriffs and officers; it was an exposition of Romans xiv. 10, and he called it 'The Great Assize'. It is divided into three parts: events which will precede and lead up to the judgment, in which is included a vivid picture of Christ coming with clouds; a description of the judgment scene itself; and finally a description of the things which must certainly follow. He then closes by exhorting his hearers to repentance and faith. 'The judge of all is likewise the Saviour of all. Hath He not bought you with His own blood, that you might not perish, but have everlasting life? O make proof of His mercy, rather than of His justice; of His love, rather than the thunder of His power.'[1]

[1] *Sermons*, vol. i, p. 205.

CHAPTER IX

'EVEN SO, COME, LORD JESUS'

WE began this study by seeking what justification the Scripture affords for an assurance that Jesus Christ will one day come again, visibly and in person, as Christians have always believed and have embodied in their Creed. We discovered that the evidence was abundant, and that from the beginning this belief was held as a fundamental of the faith. Moreover, as we looked more closely at the words of promise, we discovered that these not only held out to us a living hope for the future, but contained teaching of real importance for the present, which we needed to know and put into practice. Bound up with belief in the Advent was the duty of taking heed in view of false teachers and seducing spirits, of being zealous in world evangelization, of watchfulness and prayer, and a seeking after greater holiness of life. We proceeded to face problems, complex and difficult, as to the time, near or distant, and as to the manner of the Advent; and of these we found available some partial solutions, at the same time having humbly to confess the limitations of our finite understanding.

We then turned to the last book of the Bible, difficult but of entrancing interest, where we saw the veil drawn back, a door opened in heaven and wondrous pictures of the victorious Lamb of God. We learned from it more about the approaching end of the age and what might follow. From this we gave more detailed consideration to the prophecy it contains of the binding of Satan for a thousand years, to the promises to Israel and the possibilities connected with the recent establishment of the State of Israel. Again the words 'Watch and pray' pointed us to our duty.

Our Lord's exhortation to 'take heed' was then applied to warn us against the great enemy of our souls, who is no less the enemy of Jesus Christ, waging a constant warfare against Him and His followers, one likely to be more fierce as the Advent approaches. Finally, we sought to interpret the words of our Creed, 'From thence He shall come to judge the quick and the dead', and to prepare ourselves to face that judgment. In so doing we were reminded that judgment is only one side of the coin, the other is salvation. As we assure ourselves of our faith in Jesus Christ, and our perfect redemption in Him, we realize that for us as believers, the Advent of our Saviour is a lively hope, and beyond it lies a glorious future. And Jesus Himself is the centre of this hope.

THE REVELATION OF JESUS CHRIST

When John wrote down his visions, which he saw in the Isle of Patmos, he entitled his book 'the revelation of Jesus Christ'. It is this in a double sense, for it was His, and He signified it to John by His angel; and secondly, in it Jesus was revealed, His person, His glory, and His coming in victory. Here His divinity shines forth; He shares the Father's throne (Rev. v. 6, xxii. 3) and the Father's attribute of eternity (i. 8, 11; xxii. 13). Yet He never ceases to be man, the Son of man, retaining His earthly name of Jesus, and His human origin, the root and offspring of David (xxii. 16).

A second fundamental truth, that He shed His blood as the atonement for our sins, is also revealed, both in plain statement (i. 5, v. 9) and in the retention throughout the book of the symbol of the Lamb that was slain, even from the foundation of the world, and to all eternity. Thus it reveals Jesus Christ as He is and in His coming glory.

What is true of this one book is true of the whole Bible. When Jesus opened the Scriptures of the Old Testament to Cleopas and his companion on the first Easter day (Lk. xxiv. 27), Moses, the prophets and the psalms were all shown to be a revelation of the things concerning Himself. Thus Jesus is revealed in the Old Testament as the Messiah, in the Gospels as the Son of God and the Son of man, in the Epistles as the indwelling Christ, and in the Apocalypse as the ascended Lord, the Lamb on the throne.

But the revelation is not complete, for we shall yet see Him face to face, when He comes with power and glory. What a vision that will be! A few years ago a little Muslim child in a C.M.S. Sunday School in Palestine had been looking at some illustrations of the gospel story. On the following morning she greeted her teacher with a beaming face. 'Oh Sitt; last night I saw Jesus in a dream and He is a hundred times better than the pictures!' We likewise believe that a revelation of Jesus Christ awaits us at His coming, and that the vision of Him as He is will far exceed all that we have hitherto been able to conceive.

We have seen the glory of an autumn sunset, and, some of us, the sun rising in the fullness of its strength above the horizon of an eastern sea. Such glories are but a foretaste of the day when we shall see 'the Sun of righteousness arise with healing in his wings' (Mal. iv. 2). It is true that already 'God hath shined in our hearts, to give the light of the knowledge of the glory of God in the face of Jesus Christ' (2 Cor. iv. 6). But often the shining of that light has been faint and dim.

It will be different at the Advent, for then Jesus will come with power, and we shall be changed. Then our faculties will be enlarged, vistas will be opened to us, and problems solved, which now are beyond our grasp. 'Ay,' said Browning, 'but a man's reach is beyond his grasp,—else, what's a heaven for?' Let this thought stir us to mental and spiritual activity. 'Gird up the loins of your mind, be sober, and hope to the end for the grace that is to be brought unto you at the revelation of Jesus Christ' (1 Pet. i. 13). On this verse Alan Stibbs comments,[1] 'Such sure and radiant expectation should be an unfailing mark of the believer in Christ.'

HE WILL COME TO REIGN

And when Jesus comes in His glory, He will come to reign. At His first coming Jesus was 'born King of the Jews' (Mt.

[1] *Commentary on* 1 *Peter* (Tyndale Press, 1959), p. 85.

ii. 2). By this title His Messiahship was made known to
the three wise men, and it was this that struck fear into the
heart of Herod. His advent was preceded by a long time of
promise and prophecy. God, having found in David a man
after His own heart, set him on the throne of Israel, and
promised him a son, and sent Nathan the prophet with a
promise to stablish the throne of his kingdom for ever (2 Sa.
vii. 13). But Israel and Judah rebelled against the Lord, who
allowed their enemies to triumph over them and carry them
into captivity. Yet even in the dark days of King Zedekiah,
Jeremiah prophesied of a future when the Lord would raise
up to David a righteous Branch, a king who should reign and
prosper (Je. xxiii. 5). Jerusalem fell, king and people were
carried into captivity, and among them a well favoured youth
named Daniel. God enabled him to recall and interpret a
dream of Nebuchadnezzar, and in later years a vision of a
Son of man who came with the clouds of heaven to whom
was given a kingdom both universal and everlasting (Dn. ii. 44,
vii. 13f.). Through many vicissitudes the messianic hope
lingered in Israel. Jesus was indeed the Christ, as Simon Peter
confessed (Mt. xvi. 16f.); but not the earthly king for whom
they looked. 'My kingdom is not of this world,' He said to
Pilate (Jn. xviii. 36).

Today Jesus reigns in heaven at His Father's side; there 'we
see Jesus . . . crowned with glory and honour' (Heb. ii. 9).
And He reigns in the hearts of those whom He has redeemed
out of every tribe and nation; yet He is rejected by the world,
which does not own either His power or His rule.

But the day is approaching, and it may be very near, when
He will come with great power and glory. Then every eye
will see Him as the Prince of the kings of the earth, and then
'every tongue shall confess that Jesus Christ is Lord' (Phil.
ii. 11), and His kingdom will be a kingdom without end.

When Handel sought a theme for his music, he found it in
Revelation xix. 1–7, in the chorus of Hallelujahs that greeted
the fall of God's enemies, and the reign of the Lord God
omnipotent. With this he combined the Advent of the King

of kings and Lord of lords, and the promise that 'he shall reign for ever and ever' (Rev. xi. 15); and what music he made!

We shall join in the chorus of praise when we see our Saviour coming, for He comes to reign. Among the wonders of that time will any be greater than this, that if we overcome, we shall share His throne? Yet this was the promise to the church in Laodicea (Rev. iii. 21), and we live in an age of Laodicean indifference and ease.

OUR PRESENT DUTY

But can we qualify for this? Do we live an overcoming life, and do the words apply to us, 'if we suffer, we shall also reign with him'? (2 Tim. ii. 12). Let us examine ourselves.

When Peter contemplated the end of the world and the dissolution of the elements, he was led to exclaim, 'Seeing that these things are thus all to be dissolved, what manner of persons ought ye to be in all holy living and godliness, looking for and earnestly desiring the coming of the day . . .' (2 Pet. iii. 11, 12, RV). Here is a challenge which we do well to apply to ourselves; for it is easy to indulge in sentimentality or in idle speculation regarding the Lord's return, and neglect the present duty. The challenge is threefold, to character, to conduct, and to expectancy.

The challenge is first of all to 'holy living'. Let there be no mistake here; scriptural holiness is no unattainable ideal, reserved for a few choice spirits. It is a command (1 Pet. i. 16), with full provision for its fulfilment (Col. i. 22), and frequently connected with the Advent (1 Thes. iii. 13; 1 Jn. iii. 3). These references, studied alongside the exhortations in Revelation ii and iii, will help us in our search for holiness. Moreover the history of revivals shows that it has been, and still may be, the realized ideal of ordinary people, where there is an outpouring of the Holy Spirit.[1] In the present also, for while these words are being written there are hundreds of Africans in Ruanda and the surrounding countries, belonging

[1] See for example John Wesley's sermons.

to the Revival Movement, whose daily lives are a practical exposition of 1 John i. 7–ii. 2. And wherever there is a genuine revival the experience of the early Church is repeated, and it is discovered that a life of practical holiness is indeed possible, and that the whole spirit and soul and body may be preserved blameless unto the coming of the Lord Jesus Christ (1 Thes. v. 23). Character and conduct are inseparable. The thought of heart cleansing in 1 John i. 9 leads quickly on to the atonement and the need of 'the whole world', and the Lord Himself taught that His sufferings and glory were in order that repentance and remission of sins should be preached in His name among nations (Lk. xxiv. 47).

The connection between the Advent and world evangelization has been discussed.[1] It is not enough that we should recognize this as a doctrine, we must take an active share in it, by personal witness and endeavour, by substantial gifts to missionary work, and by earnest and intelligent prayer. By so doing we hasten the Lord's coming.

The Advent also calls for expectancy in the Christian; it is a hope which affects our *personal relationship* with Jesus Christ. Luther once said, truly enough, that Christianity is a religion of personal pronouns. Remember Jesus' words to Peter, 'What is that to thee? Follow thou me.' Is our walk then close with the Lord, so close that if He should come tomorrow it would seem natural to be with Him? Because my relationship with Him is so close, my life bound up with His, am I seeking those things which are above, where He is seated at God's right hand (Col. iii. 1)? Let us ask ourselves once again, Am I walking in the light with Him? Is Jesus Christ to me,

> A living bright reality,
> More present to faith's vision keen,
> Than any earthly object seen.

A companion of the writer, on a Mediterranean journey, found herself sharing a cabin with a young Jewish girl on her

[1] See above, pp. 24f., 36.

way to Jerusalem to be married. We got to know her and witnessed to her concerning our Saviour who was willing to be hers also. Before parting she said, 'You are the first people whom I have met to whom Christ seems *real*.' Real indeed He is, and we shall see Him soon. How wonderful it will be to experience His actual presence, His *parousia*, after His long absence from the visible world, His 'appearing after being hidden from our eyes'—and, it may be soon.

THE MIDNIGHT CRY

'And at midnight there was a cry made, Behold, the bridegroom cometh; go ye out to meet him' (Mt. xxv. 6). Why midnight? 'Because suddenly, as though at the dead of night, and when all are off their guard, the coming of Christ will resound' (Jerome). Here is the point of the parable; all alike were ignorant of the exact hour of His coming; but some were prepared for it beforehand and others not. The former had oil in their lamps; endued by the Spirit, they shine as lights in a world of darkness. The cry, 'Go ye out to meet Him', fills their heart with gladness; the great moment for which they had been preparing has come. With lamps alight and joy in their hearts, they go in with Him to the marriage.

It is thus that Jesus Himself likens His coming to a wedding, and John re-echoes the thought as the Bible nears its close, 'Let us be glad and rejoice, and give honour to him: for the marriage of the Lamb is come, and his wife hath made herself ready' (Rev. xix. 7).

On this note of readiness and rejoicing let us bring our study to a close. In the quiet of our hearts let us again share with John in his final vision. Let us listen to the Lord saying, 'Behold, I come quickly'; and let us gladly respond, 'Even so, come, Lord Jesus.'

INDEX OF SCRIPTURE REFERENCES

AUTHOR INDEX

GENERAL INDEX